Making
Wire Jewellery

Making
Wire Jewellery

Janice Zethraeus

THE CROWOOD PRESS

First published in 2016 by
The Crowood Press Ltd
Ramsbury, Marlborough
Wiltshire SN8 2HR
www.crowood.com

British Library Cataloguing-in-Publication Data
A catalogue record for this book is available from the British Library.
ISBN 978 1 78500 165 9

DEDICATION

I would like to dedicate this book to the three men in my life: my husband Bo, who is my rock and has always been an immense source of support for all my creative endeavours, and my sons Simon and Adam, whose advice and critiques I could not do without.

ACKNOWLEDGEMENTS

Thanks to Margaret Chodos-Irvine for her creative text perspectives and to the talented Catherine Hendy for her advice and the use of her ring images. A word of gratitude to Simon B. Armitt for the many photographs he has taken for this book. Finally, I am grateful to all the people in the UK jewellery world who have helped to make my second career as a jewellery designer-maker so exciting and fulfilling.

Typeset by Kelly-Anne Levey
Printed and bound in India by Replika Press Pvt Ltd.

CONTENTS

INTRODUCTION

Creating jewellery to adorn the body dates back to prehistoric times. Natural objects such as shells, stone and animal teeth have been discovered in archaeological digs across the world, some dating back nearly 100,000 years. Over time, humans began manipulating these objects, creatively fashioning wearable adornments from these raw materials. With the advent of the Bronze Age, over 5,000 years ago, metallurgy transformed jewellery making. The qualities of metal jewellery made it exceedingly desirable, being both aesthetically appealing and long-lasting.

The Sumerians and Romans are examples of ancient cultures that used wire components in their designs. The ancient Celtic and Viking cultures also provided us with numerous examples of pieces dominated by the use of metal wire.

Wire can be used in jewellery making without the need for heating and soldering. Methods such as wire wrapping, crocheting and beading can produce embellished pieces with no heat or flame. Joining metal with cold connections and the use of unsoldered links, crimps, hinges and rivets can be implemented as alternative techniques. This book, however, will focus on using soldering techniques to create wire jewellery. Soldering improves the functionality and appearance of a design: it helps provide strength and security, and also imparts a clean and finished look. A soldered jump ring will retain its strength much longer than an unsoldered one. Soldering can enable you to construct pieces that have depth and form. Hardened wire is both strong and lightweight – important factors when creating pieces with larger dimensions: a statement piece need not be cumbersome and heavy.

The satisfaction that can be derived from working with wire will depend on how one approaches jewellery making. Using fine wire requires precision and patience and can be time-consuming. Soldering is the paramount skill required when making wire jewellery. Like any creative process, it is a skill learnt by repetition, trial and error. As skills are practised, techniques are fine-tuned to suit the individual maker. Unfortunate mistakes, such as overheating and melting the metal, become fewer as time goes on. It is important to note that makers employ a range of techniques in their work and those involving forming and soldering may include short cuts developed over time. This book will offer instructions and tips that I have developed which suit my way of working. They are not the only way to approach working with wire.

Undertaking a new project and following its journey from first sketch to final piece can be frustrating, but fulfilling. Long hours spent at the bench to produce a single item of jewellery are worth the result: a unique piece of wearable art.

WIRE AS A RAW MATERIAL

Wire, purchased from bullion suppliers, can be ordered in lengths to suit one's specific design needs. A very wide range of sizes and shapes can be found. Further manipulation of the wire by twisting or hammering it or using a drawplate to make the wire thinner can provide endless variations to suit specific designs. This broad choice in both size and shape makes wire a versatile material that can be used to great advantage in jewellery making.

A variety of precious and non-precious metals can be used to produce wire. Precious metals such as gold and silver have long been the preferred choices for jewellery. The ease of soldering and working these metals makes them a perfect choice for creating pieces out of wire: the finished product will be strong and light. This enables the designer to create larger pieces of jewellery that will be both lightweight and easy to wear.

METAL ALLOYS: COPPER, SILVER AND GOLD

Copper is the oldest mineral mined by man and has been used in jewellery making for thousands of years. Although not a precious metal, its relatively low cost and properties similar to those of silver make it an ideal metal to begin working with. For the same reasons it is perfect for model making.

Before production can begin, metals must undergo annealing – the process of heating and cooling to make the material capable of manipulation. Once annealed, copper becomes extremely soft, making it malleable and easy to manipulate with pliers. The main disadvantage with copper is that it tarnishes easily and may cause skin discolouration when worn. A finished piece of copper jewellery may be plated with silver or gold if so desired.

Silver is a precious metal with great appeal. The white colour of the metal reflects light beautifully when highly polished. A matt finish will give it a pleasingly soft glow. Silver will easily enhance and complement settings of gemstones and pearls. Although more expensive than copper, making jewellery with silver is not cost-prohibitive. Silver is available in a variety of alloys, and silver wire is most often found in two qualities. Fine silver (999) is 99.9 per cent pure, but is much too soft to lend itself well to the production of wire jewellery. Jewellers tend to work with sterling silver (925), which contains 92.5 per cent silver mixed with other metals (mostly copper) to form an alloy that is stronger than fine silver but retains enough softness when annealed to make it easy to work with. The pieces of jewellery featured in this book are made with sterling silver. One disadvantage of using sterling silver is that the metal will tarnish over time, reacting to exposure to oxygen in the air. This issue can easily be resolved by periodically polishing the jewellery.

Gold is one of the world's most precious metals, being highly valued in jewellery making for thousands of years. Pure gold (24 carat) is extremely

These rings have been made using different metal alloys: sterling silver, 9ct rose gold and 18ct yellow gold.

soft and malleable, but it is often combined with different metal alloys to be used for making jewellery. These alloys lower the purity of the gold, which results in it being described as lower in carat (abbreviated to ct). Gold alloys with a lower carat rating are a superior choice for making wire jewellery due to their increased strength and durability. Eighteen carat gold (750) contains 75 per cent gold alloyed with other metals: it will not tarnish or corrode. Fourteen carat gold (583) contains 58.3 per cent gold, and 9ct gold (375) contains 37.5 per cent. These gold alloys are very well suited to jewellery making. Because of its lower gold percentage, 9ct gold's cost makes it an increasingly attractive option when choosing a metal to work with. However, because of its high percentage of alloy metals such as copper, 9ct gold has a tendency to tarnish with time.

The colour of gold is derived from the type and percentage of alloy mixed with it. Yellow gold commonly contains copper and silver. Red or rose gold contains more copper. White gold contains more nickel. Note that the purity of the coloured gold, whether yellow, red or white, remains dependent on the quantity of gold in the piece. The colour of the gold is not an indication of its carat worth.

When selecting a metal wire to use for a new design, it is advisable to look at the characteristics and benefits of the different alloys. The choice of using copper, silver or gold wire will depend to some extent on the maker's budget and preferred colour of the final piece, but it is not the only factor. It is also important to consider where on the body one will wear the item of jewellery. For instance, a brooch or pendant, which is not worn close to the skin, may have different requirements in metal purity and quality from an earring stud or ring which has close contact with the skin.

METAL HARDNESS

Metal hardness refers to the malleability of a metal; that is, how easily it will bend. Bullion suppliers offer wire in varying degrees of hardness: hard-conditioned, half-hard-conditioned and soft, fully annealed wire. Hard-conditioned wire is extremely stiff and will not easily bend, making it unsuitable for use if a design requires curved forms. Half-hard wire, though less stiff, is not easily manipulated. As heat will be introduced during soldering, making the wire soft in the process, it makes sense to begin with soft, fully annealed wire. It is pliable, making it easy to form curves, jump rings and other forms.

As stress is applied to the wire during the course of jewellery making, it becomes toughened. The term 'work-hardened' is used to describe this process. Twisting, hammering, burnishing and pulling wire through a drawplate or placing a finished piece in a barrel polisher will work-harden the wire, making it stiffer and stronger. During jewellery production the wire can be re-annealed, if necessary, to make it soft again (*see* Chapter 4 for instruction on annealing).

Burnishing is one way to work-harden wire.

WIRE: VARIATIONS OF SIZE AND SHAPE

Wire can be purchased in a variety of shapes and thicknesses (gauges). Silver wire, which is the predominant choice for jewellery making, offers the greatest variety of choice. The gauge of ready-made wire can range from as fine as 0.4mm to over 5mm in width. Most jewellery referenced in this book is made from wire between 0.7mm and 3mm wide. Wire that is very fine will not be robust enough to hold its shape when hardened and wire in a very heavy gauge will be extremely difficult to form. If a desired width of wire cannot be sourced, a thicker wire can be drawn down to the preferred size by using a drawplate (*see* Chapter 4).

The most common shapes of ready-made wire are round, square, rectangular, oval and D-shape. When creating an intricate piece of wire jewellery, the jeweller may choose to use round wire, as it is quicker to work with in comparison to square or rectangular wire. In the symmetrical profile of round wire there is no 'top and bottom' to consider. For a crisp design, square- and rectangular-shaped wire require alignment before soldering, and if used, care must be taken so that the edges are not dented or twisted during the making process.

If you are interested in using a more decorative wire in a design, or want to highlight or embellish a piece, a variety of shapes can be sourced from shops that supply jewellery-making materials. Bead wire, twisted wire and patterned wire can be found in an array of sizes and styles. Alternatively, you can easily manipulate wire with hammers or twist it by hand (*see* Chapter 4).

Wire can be sourced in a variety of gauges and shapes.

Examples of decorative wire include single and double twisted wire, hammered wire and bead wire purchased from bullion suppliers.

INSPIRATION AND DESIGN

The inspiration for every jewellery designer is a very personal matter. Observations from the world around us (including images, dreams, and even music) have an impact on the senses, motivating creativity. Past experiences and the way one approaches new experiences influence the perspective of the designer and cause ideas to evolve. The interpretation of a design is subjective, with infinite variations and combinations. Two people will interpret the same inspiration on a very personal level, which accounts for the innumerable varieties of designs.

As personal as inspiration can be, there are a few recurrent themes that have been chosen by artists through the ages. The natural world has been a favourite subject for designers since humans began to create jewellery. A desire to capture the essence of or interpret an aspect of natural beauty has encouraged jewellers from all cultures. Shell, leaf and flower motifs echo through thousands of years of jewellery design. Contemporary jewellery design has also had strong influences from architecture and geometric patterns. Straight lines and angular shapes, not often found in nature, can form a striking basis for designs.

Finding your own inspiration is key to designing an original collection of jewellery. Together with one's choice of material and construction techniques, this will ensure that the finished pieces will be interesting and distinctive.

THE DESIGN PROCESS

The design process is individual and varies widely between designers. Collecting images in a visual diary can provide a starting point. Carry a small notebook and camera to document observations that attract your attention. Gather together photographs and clippings from magazines and

Take photographs of interesting objects that inspire you and save them for future reference in a visual diary.

Collected objects can provide great inspiration.

newspapers, either in digital or paper format. Save objects of interest discovered during activities such as beachcombing, walks taken in the countryside or even day-to-day pursuits. Together, these steps can help inform your choices and communicate your ideas as you proceed with your designs, as a personal perspective will add interest and depth to the finished product.

When deciding what to design, there are two important practical considerations to be made about the piece: the form and the function. A bangle, ring, neckpiece or brooch will each require different considerations regarding the size of the item and the materials used to make it. Its weight and sturdiness are important to think about. The thickness and shape of the chosen wire will affect the robustness of the final piece. Is the piece intended for daily use? Bangles and rings are more prone to rougher contact during daily wear: a heavier wire could be preferable from that standpoint. A cocktail ring worn on special occasions may be more delicate in design. Weight is a particular factor when producing earrings: wire is relatively light and can enable a designer to go for big impact without making the earrings uncomfortable to wear. Think about your priorities for the finished piece and design accordingly.

An assortment of pens, rulers and templates can be useful, particularly when drawing detailed or technical sketches.

The type of material chosen for making the jewellery and the construction techniques that will be used should be considered during the design process. Using wire to make jewellery will dictate to a certain degree what techniques, such as soldering, are necessary for fabrication. The addition of other elements in the design and the material they are made from can affect the way one integrates them into the piece. For example, gems and pearls need to be introduced at the end of production, as they cannot be exposed to heat in the process of soldering. It is helpful to be aware of any limitations in your choice of materials, in order to creatively find ways to work around these restrictions.

SKETCHING AND PLANNING

Keeping a sketchbook is invaluable. It enables you to collect and reference different ideas and options when designing. It will document your progression as the design evolves. Avoid discarding rejected designs as they may come in handy for future projects.

Equip yourself with the drawing tools with which you feel most comfortable. You may choose a variety of pencils, markers and pens to use in your sketchbook. A ruler can be helpful in estimating the length of wire that will be needed to produce a piece. Templates can be sourced in both round and oval shapes: these will greatly assist in sketching clean curves.

Sketches can provide a useful record of the design process.

MODEL MAKING

Many designers find model making a useful step when designing jewellery. Making models with copper wire is an ideal way to start the 3-D process. When annealed, copper is very soft and easy to manipulate. Creating trial pieces using copper wire and silver solder will help visualize the design options available. These pieces may not have a beautiful colour or surface finish, but they provide an important function. They are extremely useful to help test different options of wire length and width. In assisting the evolution of the design process, they will inform the choices made to achieve the final look. Avoid the temptation to throw away unresolved models. A first attempt, which might be deemed unsuccessful, may be a useful reference later on, even for a different project.

TEST PIECES

The next step in the design process is to produce a test piece. This is especially recommended when working with more complicated designs. Producing a trial piece can help to work out any queries in regards to form and weight. It will also help in deciding which gauge of wire to choose for the final design. Any weaknesses in the design can be analysed and improved upon. Producing a test piece can help save money, especially if you plan on using a more expensive metal, such as 18ct gold, in the final design. Trial and error with silver wire will help contribute to a more successful and economic result in a gold wire finished piece.

Making a test piece will also enable you to give the jewellery a 'trial run'. It is important to see how the piece relates to the body and how it

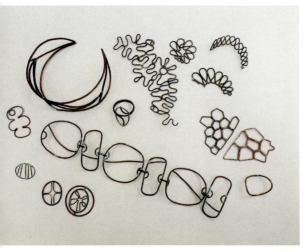

Copper models help to visualize design options.

Test pieces lend valuable information to the design process.

feels when worn. Is the design functional? In the case of a necklace, are you satisfied with how it hangs, its balance and weight? Using a mannequin is ideal when accessing a necklace design.

Is the bracelet or cuff a good fit on the wrist? Are the earrings comfortable to wear? All decisions made at this stage will improve upon the final design.

A mannequin can be useful in assessing how a neckpiece will hang on the body.

STUDIO AND EQUIPMENT

Wire is a versatile medium for jewellery making. This raw material is easy to source, with a wide range of price points for different metals to suit individual budgets. Starting to work with wire can be done with a minimum investment in tools: one can start with the basic necessities and improve upon the quality and selection as time goes by. Jewellery-making tools can be expensive and putting together a complete collection can be very costly. However, new, cutting-edge tools are not always necessary, especially when starting out. Purchasing second-hand tools can be an excellent way of building up a stock of the essentials.

Although an organized and well-equipped studio space is a joy to work in, you can start in modest surroundings. The safety of your working environment is paramount: jewellery making requires a soldering torch, so any fire risk should be a primary concern when setting up a work area. Good lighting, a power supply, good ventilation and easy access to water are all necessities when considering a workspace. Natural lighting is preferable, but direct sunlight is best avoided as it can interfere with your ability to see the flame when soldering. Complement overhead lighting with a lamp mounted on or near the bench, which can be directed on the work.

A jeweller's bench can be customized to suit the individual maker.

AT THE BENCH

A jeweller's bench is an essential investment for jewellery making, as its height and design provides a comfortable and productive work area. A traditional jeweller's bench is equipped with a semi-circular surface with a bench peg centrally mounted, below which a bench skin or drawer is positioned to collect small bits of metal and filings.

The bench peg is a wedge-shaped piece of wood with a horizontal surface and a slanted surface. The peg is notched with a 'V' in the centre and mounted onto the bench with the slanted surface on the top. A securely mounted bench peg will support your work as you file and

Bench peg secured to the table with a G-clamp.

A vernier gauge accurately measures the width of wire.

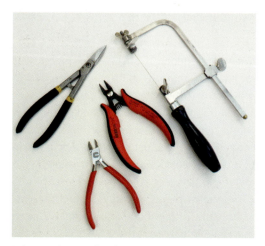

Wire-cutting tools: shears, side cutters, flush cutters and adjustable saw frame.

sand. The notch in the peg can be cut to a shape and size to suit yourself and can be modified to suit special tasks if necessary. If you are new to jewellery making, try setting up a small stable table using a simple G-clamp to attach a bench peg. This can be an easy and inexpensive way to start working before deciding to invest in a proper jeweller's bench.

WIRE CUTTING

Working with wire, especially in complicated designs, entails a great deal of cutting. Cutting with precision is advantageous, especially when using more expensive wire, as there will be less waste. A few simple tools will benefit the process.

- Fine permanent marker: this is useful for marking out metal. It is less likely to smudge when handling the wire.
- Metal ruler.
- Vernier gauge: this tool enables accurate measuring of wire diameter and could be either traditional steel or digital format.
- Dividers: steel dividers help measure precise wire lengths and accurately find the centre of a circle.
- Shears: although these are not ideal for cutting wire, they are useful for cutting sheet and solder strip.
- Side cutters and flush cutters: the former are necessary tools for wire cutting; the latter are similar but more precise and perfect for cutting lower-gauge wire, as they leave a flatter surface on the cut side of the wire.
- Adjustable saw frame and saw blades: use an adjustable saw for cutting heavy-gauge and square wire. Blades come in a variety of sizes, usually in bundles of 12: grade 2/0 is a good size to start with.
- Beeswax: this is a useful lubricant for use on saw blades to achieve smoother cutting.

FILING, SHAPING, TEXTURING

The following items are part of a jeweller's basic toolkit and helpful for working with wire.

- Steel bench block, also known as a flat stake. This hard plate provides an excellent surface when using a hammer or mallet to form or texture wire. A clean and polished surface will ensure that no marks will be transferred to the wire during use.
- Hammers and mallets. Metal hammers are useful for tapering and texturing wire: different shaped heads will produce a variety of textures. Rawhide mallets have a softer head and will shape and flatten wire without marking it: these are essential for use with metal mandrels and triblets.
- Bangle mandrel. These can be purchased in both round and oval shapes. Metal mandrels are heavy, with a flat bottom and are used free standing. Wooden mandrels have a handle, which can be secured in a vice.
- Ring mandrel, also known as a triblet. Round triblets are used to form precise rings of various sizes. Oval-shaped triblets can also be very useful. Triblets are made of steel and can be held in the hand or secured in a vice.
- Doming block and punches. Doming punches come in various sizes and can be useful in helping form wire components into domed shapes.
- Pliers: these are essential tools for manipulating wire and come in many varieties, including round-nose, flat-nose, snipe-nose, parallel and half-round.
- Files, both flat and half-round, are especially useful for filing heavy-gauge wire. Files come in a variety of cuts (coarseness): the most common, cut 2, is usually sufficient for wirework.
- Needle files: these are much smaller than the ordinary flat and half-round and they come in a large variety of shapes and cuts. A set of

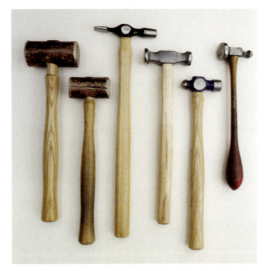

Selection of hammers and mallets including leather mallets, cross-pein hammer, planishing hammer, ball-pein hammer and repoussé hammer.

Metal mandrels and triblets.

needle files is essential for more detailed work with wire. A set of cut 2 files can be complemented with one or two files in a coarser cut of 0 if desired. Common shapes include round, half-round, flat, warding, three-square and square. A safety back file, which has a smooth raised ridge on one side, is indispensable for filing intricate wirework. Riffler files come in a variety of shapes and can be useful for filing hard-to-reach areas.

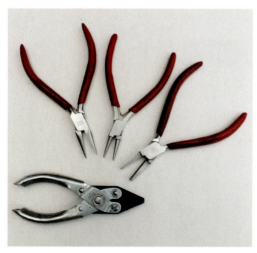

Selection of pliers: snipe-nose, round-nose, half-round and parallel pliers.

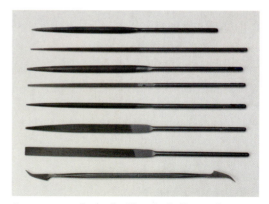

Assortment of needle files, including safety back, round, half-round, square, three-square, flat, warding and riffler files.

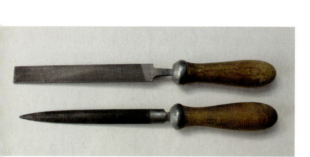

Flat and half-round files are useful for working with heavy-gauge wire.

Example of a second-hand vice.

- Drawplates are used to reduce the gauge of wire. They are available with holes of different sizes and shapes so choose one that suits your specific need.
- Vice: a simple, general-purpose vice has many uses.

SOLDERING AND PICKLING

Precision soldering is key when working with wire, and the most important item of all your tools is the soldering torch. A hand-held butane torch is perfect for beginners. Easy to use and inexpensive, it can be purchased from hardware stores and jewellery equipment suppliers. A small butane canister provides quick refills. The flame produced is small and relatively weak but is soft and ideal for annealing small items. However, it can be insufficient for soldering designs where a precise and strong flame is needed.

Many jewellers use Sievert torches, which operate on propane. These torches are well adapted to a variety of soldering jobs of different sizes. Interchangeable nozzles provide a degree of choice regarding the size of the flame. However, some jewellers feel the flame may not be fine enough for especially intricate work.

For especially fine soldering jobs, a micro welder is an expensive but ideal investment if

Hand-held butane torch.

A micro welder is perfect for soldering intricate designs.

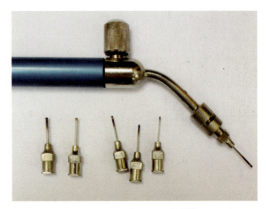

Choosing between torch tips of different sizes alters the size and strength of the flame.

you intend to spend a great amount of time soldering wire. Not to be confused with a laser welder or PUK welder, this is a type of torch that is used for soldering. It is a gas-generating torch unit that produces hydrogen and oxygen by electrolysis using distilled water. The gas burns as it is being produced, so there is no need to store gas canisters. This makes the micro welder a safe choice. Its flame is extremely hot and precise, which is perfect when working on more complex designs where heating a specific area of the piece is preferred. Interchangeable nozzle tips of different sizes will enable you to regulate the size of the flame.

The other essential items for this process are as follows.

• Lighter or matches. A lighter is not needed if using a hand-held butane torch, as it is equipped with an automatic igniter (a spark is produced as the trigger is pressed). A small hand-held lighter is useful for lighting a larger torch or micro welder. Some jewellers prefer to use matches as they find them safer.

• Fireproof bricks: these are used to support the piece that will be soldered. A small fireproof area that can be reconfigured depending on the size and design of the piece is ideal. Honeycomb boards can also be used, as they enable air to circulate easily around the piece during soldering, creating a more even distribution of heat.

Essential soldering equipment includes fireproof bricks, tweezers, reverse-action tweezers, solder probe and third hand.

A slow cooker is a practical appliance to use as a pickling tank.

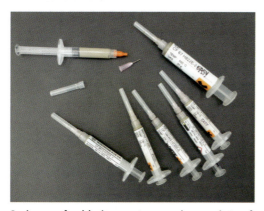

Syringes of soldering paste come in a variety of grades and colours.

- Stainless steel tweezers: small, precise tweezers will help with moving and manipulating solder and wire.
- Reverse-action tweezers: these are very useful, as they will hold and support the work while soldering. The insulated wooden grips do not conduct much heat and make the tweezers easy to handle during and after the soldering process.
- Solder probe: the sharp point of this tool is used to help position solder during the heating process.
- Third hand: these reverse-action tweezers are mounted on a stand and can be easily pivoted and positioned. Two can be used when working with complex designs.
- Pickling powder: dissolving this powder in water produces a corrosive solution that will remove flux and oxides after the soldering process. Also known as safety pickle, it is ideal for use with silver and gold. A non-toxic type of picking powder is also available for use with copper and silver.
- Pickle tank or slow cooker: a glass or ceramic receptacle can be used to hold the pickle solution. However, keeping the pickle solution warm will speed the process of removing flux residue and oxides. A small slow cooker is inexpensive and will keep the solution at the desired temperature in a safe manner. Always turn off a slow cooker when not in use.
- Pickle basket: a small basket is useful, especially when pickling small items. This will hold smaller pieces such as jump rings in the pickle, enabling easy and quick removal.
- Brass or plastic tweezers: never use steel tweezers when removing items from the pickle, as they will contaminate the solution.
- Quench/rinsing cup: a ceramic container filled with tap water can be used to quench hot, soldered wire. Additionally, after an item has been removed from the pickle, it can be dipped in the water to rinse off the picking solution.

HAND-MADE PICKLE BASKET

This basket will save a great deal of time when finding and retrieving very small items from the pickle. A simple pickle basket can be easily constructed from a plastic container such as the cap of a spray can. Punch or drill many small holes into the top of the cap to allow for good drainage. Turn it upside down and add a small handle using copper wire.

Hand-made pickle basket made from a plastic spray can cap.

- Solder and flux. Solder can be purchased in three forms: sheet, wire and paste. The preference for solder type varies depending on the individual and the job at hand. When using solder in the form of sheet and wire, it is necessary to cut the sheet or wire into small pieces, called pallions, and add flux during the soldering process. Borax, tenacity and soldering fluid are among the types of flux often used.
- I personally prefer solder paste for working with wire. As the flux is an integral part of the paste, I find this option both saves me time and gives me more control when soldering. Purchase paste to complement the type of metal chosen for the piece of jewellery. Silver solder comes in different grades: easy, medium and hard. This refers to the melting temperature of the solder. Gold solder is available in different colours as well as the three different grades. Yellow, red and white gold solders are available for both 9ct and 18ct gold.

DRILLING, POLISHING AND FINISHING

- Pendant motor. Useful for a multitude of tasks, a pendant motor can be used for drilling, sanding and polishing. A variety of accessories such as burrs, pendant wheels, drill bits and split mandrels can be attached, depending on the job needed.
- Drill bits: drills of different sizes can be used with the pendant motor.
- Split mandrel: attached to the pendant motor, a split mandrel is used to hold wet and dry paper and is used to sand metal. Strips of wet and dry paper are threaded through the slit and wound around the mandrel.
- Wet and dry paper: this is used to sand metal to remove scratches and marks in preparation for polishing. This type of paper, unlike paper that is used to sand wood, can be used either wet or dry. It comes in various

Ring clamp and wedge.

Straight burnisher.

grades, based on the size of the grit: the higher the number the finer the grit. Grades of paper are 240, 320, 400, 600, 800 1000 and 1200.

- Radial abrasive disks: attached to the pendant motor, these flexible disks help to remove scratches and polish hard-to-reach areas.
- Centre punch: this tool is used to make an indent in metal. This is helpful in keeping a drill bit in the proper place when drilling.

SECOND-HAND TOOLS

A larger tool such as a pendant motor can be an expensive investment. Purchasing second-hand tools can be a good way to start outfitting your studio, especially when the initial investment for a new tool can seem too high. Good-quality tools, even when second-hand, can have a long working life and can be upgraded when the need arises. Sometimes a tool's life expectancy can surpass expectations. This pendant motor was manufactured in the 1970s and is an example of a second-hand tool that continues function well despite its age.

Pendant motor from the 1970s.

- Ring clamp with wedge: a ring clamp is useful not only for holding rings but also for helping to hold other small items securely when filing and polishing.
- Burnisher: this tool can be sourced in straight and curved shapes and is used to highlight edges of metal and work-harden wire.
- Barrel polisher, steel shot and barrelling compound. A barrel polisher is an indispensable tool in the workshop: it is a timesaving and practical way to harden and polish wire jewellery. The jewellery is tumbled with steel shot in a mixture of water and barrelling compound. As the barrel tumbles, the steel shot collides with the wire, lubricated by the barrelling compound. The mixed-shaped shot will polish most hard-to-reach areas. When purchasing a barrel polisher, consider the size of the tumbler. The dimensions will need to be sufficient for the size of jewellery you would like to tumble.
- Finishing materials. Several different substances can be used to add decorative finishes to jewellery, ranging from household materials to solutions produced especially for jewellery making (*see* Chapter 8 for a detailed list of finishing materials).

PROTECTIVE CLOTHING

It is vital that you make your working environment comfortable and safe. Investing in the necessary equipment will help prevent unnecessary accidents.

- It is essential to use eye protection when working with a pendant motor. Safety spectacles are light yet will protect you from other hazards such as sharp objects, flying metal and dust and the wayward end of a spool of wire.
- Secure long hair and remove or tuck in items of loose clothing. Loose hair falling into a

flame or getting caught in a pendant motor when drilling or polishing can be very dangerous.

- Wearing an apron is advisable when working at the bench. If you drop hot metal or sharp objects while working, it will help protect you against injury. It will also protect clothing from safety pickle, which can damage fabrics.
- Always wear shoes to help protect feet and toes. Triblets and mandrels can be quite heavy and can cause injury if dropped.
- A dust mask should be worn when drilling, sanding and polishing.
- Always protect your hands when working with oxidizing solution.

PRACTICAL TIPS AT THE BENCH

- It is a good idea to keep the bench and work area tidy: it saves time to have quick access to tools while working.
- Good posture at the bench is important; get up and stretch from time to time, as physical well-being and relaxation will help creativity. Try to minimize rushing about.
- Be consistent when sitting down to the bench or leaving it at the end of the day. Collect loose tools at the end of a work session and put them away in their proper place. Loose wire and findings should be sorted and stored in individual plastic bags: label them clearly so that you can see their size and shape at a glance.
- Always be sure to switch off electrical appliances at the end of a workday or before a lunch break: this is especially important when using a pickle tank or slow cooker.

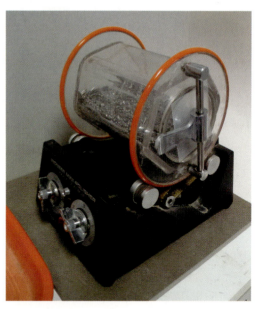

A barrel polisher safely polishes and work-hardens wire jewellery.

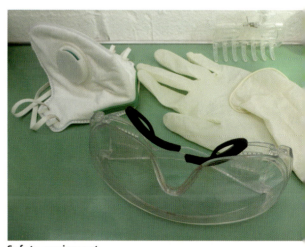

Safety equipment.

WIRE-WORKING PROCESSES

The process of making an item of wire jewellery is a combination of a variety of steps; cutting the wire, shaping, soldering and sanding it. A successful outcome depends on mastering some basic, but essential, skills. The quality of the finished piece will reflect the amount of care taken in each step of the making process.

CUTTING THE WIRE

To enable easy soldering and create a clean finish to the soldered joint, the wire should be cut or filed to a smooth, flat surface. A side cutter compresses the wire as it cuts and leaves a slightly distorted profile. This can be remedied by filing the surface flat: take care to remove any excess edges left after filing as they can create an uneven solder joint. Using a flush cutter is preferable, and is less time-consuming as it will produce a solder-ready surface, especially when used on wire with a width of 2mm or less. Caution should be taken when cutting wire; as already mentioned, it is advisable to wear safety spectacles. Start by measuring and marking the length of wire required, using a fine permanent marker. After making a cut with the flush cutter, the end of the remaining length of wire will be pinched and distorted. Remove this by snipping the end, taking care to gather the excess to recycle as scrap.

The flush cutter on the right produces a much cleaner cut to the wire when compared to a side cutter.

RECYCLING OFFCUTS AND FILINGS

When working with wire, there will be a certain degree of waste as one cuts, snips and files the material. The amount of metal can quickly add up, and salvaging and recycling the scrap is cost-efficient and easy to do. Collect the bench scraps, including sweeps or lemel (the metal dust created when sawing and filing) that have fallen into the bench skin or drawer. Always sweep the bench skin after using different types of metals, storing gold and silver separately. Save the scrap and sweeps in a rigid container, not a plastic bag, as sharp scrap can cause tears in the plastic. Some bullion suppliers provide a recycling service, the cost depending on the quality and quantity of scrap. The scrap is melted, refined and analysed and after deducting a fee you will receive cash or credit, based on the day's metal prices, to put forward to new bullion purchases.

USING A SAW FRAME

Cutting heavier wire or rod is best achieved using an adjustable saw frame. For wire with a 2mm to 4mm width, a medium saw blade in size 2/0 works well. Vary the size of blade depending

Inserting a blade into the saw frame.

Using the bench peg for support, position the saw close to eye level.

on the thickness of the wire, using a heavier grade of blade if necessary. Take care to use eye protection when using a saw frame.

To use an adjustable saw frame, you will first need to mount the saw blade. Start by ensuring that the frame is at the desired length and tighten the outer screw securely. The frame's opening should be about 100mm longer than the length of the blade. Next, insert the blade into the top of the saw with the teeth facing the outside. Always place the blade into the saw with the teeth pointing down toward the handle. Running a finger very gingerly along the blade will help determine the direction of the teeth. Tighten the screw snugly by hand. Positioning the saw frame onto the bench peg, lean into the frame so it flexes. Insert the other end of the blade into the bottom of the frame, and tighten the screw while the frame is flexed. The aim is to put a degree of tension into the blade so that it is extremely taut without any wobble. The blade should make a pinging sound when plucked with the finger.

Before starting to cut the wire, lubricate the blade by running it through a piece of beeswax to help smooth the movement. Measure and mark the wire to be cut, placing it against a bench peg and holding it firm and steady. Holding the saw frame vertically, make small downward strokes with the saw, carefully making a small mark in the metal. Continue with a steady up-and-down motion, although the blade will only be cutting on the downward stroke. If you want a square cut, it is important to hold the wire at 90 degrees to the blade, although a slight variation from a right angle can be rectified with filing.

The cut should be made without putting much pressure on the blade, as it is the movement of the teeth over the metal that cuts the wire, not hard force. Smooth motions will help prevent blade breakage. When the blade breaks, and if the break is close enough to one of the blade's ends, the remaining piece can be replaced into the saw frame, adjusting the length of the frame to suit the new length of the blade.

FILING WIRE

The coarseness or cut of a file is determined by the size of its teeth. The larger the teeth of the file, the coarser the cut will be. Using a coarse-cut file will make filing quicker but the marks left on the metal will be more pronounced and will take longer to remove with wet and dry paper. If a large amount of metal needs to be removed by filing, starting with a coarse-cut file and following with a finer-cut one can help save time.

Using the bench peg for support, hold the wire securely and file using pressure on the forward stroke only. Decrease pressure on the backward stroke. Position the wire and file at the required angle. Small pieces of wire may be fiddly to hold steady with the fingers. Using a ring clamp to hold the wire in position can be helpful.

Resting the wire on the bench peg, file using forward motions.

ANNEALING

In order to form wire, it is necessary for the metal to be soft and pliable: that is, in an annealed state. Bending the wire will be very difficult if it is in a hardened state. Also, if the metal is too hard it may crack during the process of shaping. Purchasing fully annealed wire will allow you to bypass this process. However, it will sometimes be necessary to anneal during making as the wire may become work-hardened through hammering, bending or when using a drawplate.

If using a long length of wire, it is best to coil it to allow for an even distribution of heat. Care must be taken to not overheat and melt the wire. Using a hand-held butane torch will produce a soft and bushy flame that will assist in slowly heating the metal to the required temperature. It is important to be able to see the colour change in the metal as it heats up, so avoid working in direct sunlight, preferably dimming any bright lights. Place the wire on a

Anneal wire in shorter lengths or coils on fireproof bricks.

fireproof brick and gently move the flame along the piece or coil of wire, distributing the heat over the piece. Keep moving the flame, being careful not to overheat a specific area. The wire will slowly change colour until the metal glows a dull cherry red. At this stage, remove the flame and extinguish the torch. After a few seconds, pick up the wire with insulated tweezers and quench it in a container of water.

Annealing copper is quite straightforward as it is difficult to melt with a butane torch. Silver and gold require a more careful approach as these metals have a lower melting point and may distort much more readily with too high a temperature.

Silver will become very shiny just before it is about to melt, so it is important to learn to remove the flame before reaching this point. Practising first with copper and then with pieces of scrap silver will help increase proficiency.

PICKLING

After the wire has been annealed and quenched, the surface will become discoloured. This blackened surface is the result of oxidation and can be easily removed by pickling. There are a variety of options available when choosing a pickle solution. Pickling powder, often called safety pickle, is very popular choice among jewellers and can be sourced from jewellery equipment suppliers. Mixing the powder with water forms a solution that will remove oxides and flux from copper, silver and gold. Take care when preparing the pickle solution: follow the manufacturer's instructions and always add the pickle powder to the water, not the water to the powder. Citric acid powder mixed with water and a vinegar and salt pickle are two eco-friendly alternatives that some jewellers prefer. Avoid direct contact with the skin when using pickle and dispose of any used liquid following the manufacturer's guidelines.

Although picking in cold solution will work, using heated pickling solution is a more effective and much quicker option. Pickling tanks are avail-

Jump rings in the small pickle basket.

able from jewellery equipment suppliers but a less expensive and very effective alternative is a simple slow cooker, sold in cooking appliance shops. Never use a slow cooker for both food preparation and studio work. When in use, keep the pickle at a warm temperature, never at the boiling point. Even at a relatively low heat, the solution will become stronger as the water slowly evaporates: top up with fresh water as needed. Use brass or plastic tongs, never steel, when removing items from the pickle solution. Steel will contaminate the solution and may cause a copper plate to form on silver objects subsequently placed in the pickle. After a few minutes in a warm pickle, the item of jewellery can be removed, rinsed in water and dried. It is advisable to wear eye protection when using pickle solution, as well as an apron to protect clothing.

FORMING WITH PLIERS

When working with wire it is recommended to have a collection of pliers in a variety of shapes. Choosing the correct pliers for specific jobs will help keep the wire in good condition while working it. Unsightly marks and dents will spoil the quality of a finished piece and although most marks can be filed or sandpapered away, it is easier to avoid making them in the first place.

Parallel pliers distribute their grip on the wire equally along their surface. They are particularly useful for straightening wire and bending wire at right angles. Round-nose pliers are perfect for shaping very small curves such as those of jump rings and chain. Half-round pliers work well for shaping larger curves, such as with rings. Snipe-nose pliers are useful for getting into small spaces, but care must be taken so that the edges do not leave marks. It is essential that all pliers have clean, smooth surfaces as any deeper scratches can leave marks on the annealed wire.

PERFECTLY SHAPED PLIERS

When manipulating wire into curves, round-nose or snipe-nose pliers can leave marks on the wire and half-nose pliers may not have a sufficiently rounded tip to manoeuvre comfortably. It may be desirable to alter the shape of the pliers to facilitate control. One side of these flat-nose pliers remains untouched while the other side's edges and tip have been rounded, filed and sanded smooth. This adjustment allows the wire to be supported on the flat side's surface while being curved around the rounded side. The rounded tip is narrow enough to reach into small areas.

DRAWING WIRE

Although bullion suppliers have a huge selection of wire in different shapes and gauges, it is sometimes impossible to source the correct gauge to suit the need for a specific job. The process of changing the wire's gauge by thinning it is called drawing the wire. The tools needed for this simple procedure are a drawplate, a vice and a pair of heavy pliers. Always wear eye protection when drawing lengths of wire to guard against the possibility of wayward wire ends coming into contact with the face.

A drawplate is made from steel and has a series of approximately twenty to forty holes in successively smaller sizes. Drawplates commonly have round holes, but they can also be found in other shapes such as square, oval and D-shape.

This drawplate has round holes starting at a width of 2mm.

Step by Step: Drawing Wire

1. Start with annealed wire. Using a file, shape the end of the wire into a point: this should be long enough to enable it to be gripped securely on the other side of the drawplate with the pliers.

Step 1.

2. Secure the drawplate in the vice. Insert the tapered end of the wire into the backside of the drawplate (the side with conical holes and without numbers), beginning with the hole with the snuggest fit.

Step 2.

3. Grip the wire with the pliers and pull the wire smoothly through the plate. Repeat the action of drawing the wire through the plate, decreasing the hole size each time. The wire will need to be re-annealed after a couple of draws as it will become work-hardened and prone to snapping. The point will also need to be re-filed occasionally to enable it to be threaded into the successively smaller holes with ease.

Step 3.

TWISTING WIRE

Twisted wire can be integrated into designs to create interesting decorative effects. Changing the gauge and shape of the wire will produce an assortment of patterns: for example, two round wires can be twisted together or a single square

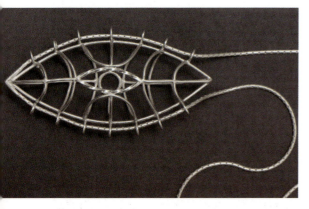

A small section of twisted square wire provides an interesting focal point on the reverse side of this pendant.

wire may be twisted alone. This process is very straightforward; all that is needed is a hand drill and a vice. Always wear eye protection when twisting lengths of wire.

Step by Step: Twisting Wire

1. Using fully annealed wire in your chosen gauge, insert the end or ends into the vice. In this example, a single wire has been folded to produce a double twist.

Step 1.

2. Secure the other end, or ends, into the jaws of the drill chuck. If twisting two wires, carefully insert them together. Make sure that you have the drill speed set correctly for the work in hand.

Step 2.

3. Start the drill and, holding the wire taut, slowly wind, continuing until the twist is as tight as required.

Step 3.

HAMMERING

Hammers and mallets are essential tools for working with wire. They can be made of a wide range of materials and shapes, and can be used for many tasks. The weight and material of the tool will determine what effect its strike will have on the metal.

A jobbing hammer, also known as a ball pein hammer, is useful for a variety of purposes. Its metal head has two ends: one is flat and the other (the ball pein) is rounded. When used in combination with a steel bench block, it can flatten, work-harden and form metal. It can also be used to add a textured or distressed finish to the wire.

Rawhide mallets are used for forming and straightening wire. Because the mallet head is made of animal hide, which is softer than the head of a metal hammer, it will shape the wire without marking or flattening it. However, if working on a steel bench block, this process will also work-harden the metal, so annealing may be required to make it soft again for further manipulation.

Rawhide mallets come in different sizes; the larger the head, the heavier the mallet will be. The smaller version is light, yet sufficient for using with finer-gauge wire. Choose a larger mallet for working with heavier wire and rod.

Texturing hammers are used to create texture and patterns. Jewellery tool suppliers provide hammers with a selection of patterns such as stripes, circles, dimples and crosses.

Use a rawhide mallet on a steel bench block to straighten smaller pieces of wire.

Making larger jump rings is straightforward when using a vice and rawhide mallet.

USING MANDRELS AND TRIBLETS

Mandrels are used to form bangles and other large round or oval shapes. They are made of either wood or hollow cast iron. While the wooden mandrels can be secured in a vice while shaping the bangle, the much heavier cast iron mandrel has a flat bottom and is used free-standing.

Triblets are basically smaller versions of the larger mandrels. They are also available in both round and oval shapes and can be obtained in various

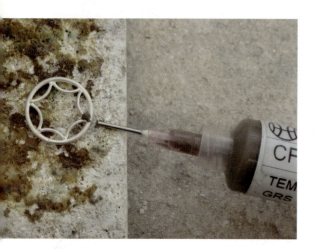

Using the correct amount of solder will help create clean solder joints.when using a vice and rawhide mallet.

sizes. The steel triblets can be hand-held or placed in a vice by the handle. On some triblets, the smooth surface may include circular marks denoting ring sizes, which is very useful when forming a ring to a precise specification. If using a marked triblet, care must be taken to avoid making marks on the inside of the formed ring.

When using metal mandrels and triblets, it is important to use only the rawhide mallet to strike the surface of the wire: in this way, you will avoid marking the metal.

SOLDERING

Careful preparation of the wire is essential for a successful solder joint. Although it is possible to rectify soldering errors, it is best to get the soldering right the first time. When soldering, it is important that the metal is clean as solder will not run properly onto metal that is dirty. In preparation for soldering, you must keep the wire free from oxidation, dust and oil. As your hands are naturally oily, care must be taken to avoid transferring oil from the skin to the wire during cutting and forming. When handling the wire, keep your hands clean and free from moisturizers.

It is very important that the surfaces to be soldered are flush. Even when using flush cutters, it may sometimes be necessary to gently file the surfaces to ensure that they fit together as tightly as possible. It can help to hold the piece up to the light to check that there is very little light shining between the two sides of the joint to be soldered.

Using the correct amount of solder is also important. Too much solder does not create a stronger joint; it only causes unsightly blobs that will need to be filed or papered away. Ideally, when completed, a soldered joint will need minimal attention and tidying up. With experience, you learn to approximate the amount of solder needed for various jobs.

Heating the piece properly when soldering is critical for controlling the flow of solder. Because the solder paste or solder pallion is smaller than the wire to be soldered, it will melt first under a direct flame. This will cause the solder to form a hot ball that will not flow properly to join the pieces. Heating the metal first, on both sides of the joint, will cause the solder to run towards the heat and seal the joint. Mastering this technique will lead to quicker and cleaner soldering results.

Fabricating and soldering rings and bangles – Step 1.

Step by Step: Fabricating and Soldering Rings and Bangles

1. Choose the shape and gauge of wire for the bangle or ring. After deciding on the desired diameter for the finished ring, take that number and multiply it by the constant pi (π), which is 3.14. This will tell you the amount of wire necessary for the circumference of the ring. The exact length needed may vary slightly depending on the gauge of the wire. Using annealed wire, measure the required length, and mark with permanent marker.

2. Cut the wire. As the width of this wire is 2mm, using a jeweller's saw will provide a cleaner cut than flush cutters, which are more suitable for lower-gauge wire.

3. Make sure that the ends are flat and square, filing if necessary.

4. Form the wire into a roughly circular shape using half-round pliers. Do not worry about making a perfect circular profile, as the soldered ring will be worked on a mandrel to ensure that it is precise. Alternatively, tap the wire around the mandrel or triblet using a rawhide mallet.

5. When the ends meet up perfectly, place the ring on the fireproof brick and add solder. Letting the joint hang slightly off the brick will maximize air circulation and can help heat the

Step 2.

Step 3.

Step 4.

Step 5.

Step 6.

Step 7.

Step 8.

Step 9.

is satisfactory before forming the ring on the mandrel.

8. Place the ring onto the mandrel. Using a rawhide mallet, tap around all sides until the ring is round. Remove the ring and turn it over, placing it again on the mandrel with the other side downward, and tap again.

9. To ensure that the ring is flat, place it on a bench block and hammer flat, using a rawhide mallet.

When soldering many solder joints simultaneously or when soldering new elements to complicated pieces, it is crucial that enough time is allotted for proper set-up and solder application. Arranging the wire components on the fireproof brick is a significant stage in the making process. Take care to ensure that the placement and angles of the wire are positioned exactly as intended before starting to solder.

pieces more quickly. Since there will only be a single solder joint, the grade of solder of choice may be easy, medium or hard.

6. Heat the entire ring slowly and then concentrate on the joint, distributing the flame on both sides. Heat the wire, not the solder.

7. When the solder has run, remove the flame. Quench the ring and pickle. Check that the joint

FIXING SOLDERING ERRORS

Occasionally, a solder joint is not satisfactory. The angle of the solder joint may be incorrect or the two ends may not be properly aligned. This should be rectified before proceeding with the piece. Sometimes it is necessary to use an adjustable saw to cut apart the faulty solder joint. Alternatively, heat can be applied to separate the pieces. Using the third hand to hold the piece securely, grasp the wire to be separated with the reverse-action tweezers. Carefully, heat the solder joint and separate the pieces, removing the flame as soon as the solder runs and the pieces separate. Quench, pickle and make sure that the ends once again are filed and meet perfectly. Solder again.

Reheat the solder joint until the solder runs and the pieces can be separated.

Being patient with set-up will help to avoid spending time correcting soldering errors.

Creating an item of jewellery with multiple joints requires planning and may take many steps of repeated soldering. Since solder will only flow properly on clean metal, some jewellers intentionally dirty parts of a piece to prevent the flow of solder in these specific areas. Correction fluid, normally used to mask errors on paper, as well as polishing rouge or graphite from a soft pencil can be applied to the metal before soldering. After soldering, these solutions should be removed before placing the item into the pickle. This technique can be useful in certain instances but generally it is preferable to use different grades of solder to control solder flow.

To prevent earlier joints from opening up when being subjected to heat for a second or third time, it can be advantageous to start by using hard or medium solder and following with easy solder. Because hard and medium solder melts at a higher temperature, these joints will remain secure as the piece is heated subsequently to the lower temperature that will allow an easy solder to run. With more soldering experience, many jewellers find this less

necessary and can solder a number of joints utilizing only one grade of solder.

An example of the use of different grades of solder can be seen with these pendants and earrings containing small decorative components. The elements on the inside of the larger circular forms need to be soldered individually before assembling them together as a group. Starting with a hard or medium solder that requires a higher melting point makes a joint that will remain solid and strong even after continuing to assemble the components using easy solder.

These flat earrings and pendants include a variety of components made with soldered wire shapes.

Soldering flat forms with multiple solder joints – Step 1.

Step 2.

Step 3.

Step 4.

Step by Step: Soldering Flat Forms with Multiple Solder Joints

1. Starting with the outside circular form, choose the shape and gauge of wire and decide on the size of the circle. In this case, the square wire has a width of 1.2mm. The diameter of the finished circle will be 24mm. To determine the length of wire needed for the circumference of the circle, multiply the diameter of 24 by 3.14 (pi/π). Measure the correct length, 75mm, and mark with permanent marker.

2. Cut the wire using flush cutters.

3. Carefully file the ends of the wire flat, as the profile will be slightly pinched.

4. Using half-round pliers, form the wire into a roughly circular shape. The square ends of the wire must be aligned perfectly.

5. Solder using hard or medium solder. Pickle the rings.

6. Form the rings on the mandrel.

7. Because the smaller elements will be on the inside of the circular form, making later clean-up difficult, filing away any excess solder will need to be done at this stage. Leave excess solder on the outside edges as this can be cleaned away at a later stage.

8. Place the large ring on a flat stake and, using a rawhide mallet, hammer flat, ensuring that the ring becomes totally level.

9. Using 0.8mm round wire, fabricate the jump rings for the small components using medium or hard solder (*see* Chapter 4 for instruction on making jump rings).

Step 5.

Step 6.

Step 7.

Step 8.

Step 9.

Step 10.

10. Manipulate the components into oval or geometric shapes if desired (*see* Chapter 6 for instruction on forming jump rings using pliers). Position the large ring on a fireproof brick and set in the smaller elements using tweezers.

11. Using easy solder, place small amounts at the junctures where the wires meet. Use the solder sparingly as any excess solder will be difficult and time-consuming to remove when the piece is finished.

12. Gently heat the piece until the solder runs. Quench, pickle and examine the junctures. If some of the connections are not joined properly, add solder and repeat the soldering process, focusing the flame on the newer connections.

13. Using needle files, tidy up any excess solder.

14. Sand away any imperfections using wet and dry paper. Finish by tumbling in the barrel polisher.

Step 11.

Step 12.

Step 13.

Step 14.

SANDING

Once an item has been soldered there may be bits of excess solder that need to be removed. If the solder lump is very large, start by using needle files of the correct shape to take away the excess, if necessary starting with a coarse-cut followed by a cut 2 file. Be cautious not to file too deeply and remove any of the wire construct. When satisfied that the surface is smooth and blemish-free, remove any remaining scratches from the filing by sanding with wet and dry paper. Some jewellers find sanding to be a tedious task, but the successful finish of a piece of jewellery largely depends on the quality of preparation of the metal before polishing.

When sanding, start with a paper with coarser grit, such as 400 or 600, depending on the depth of the scratches. Continue to sand, working through the grades to a finer grade such as 1000. Take care not to continually sand in the same direction. Instead, vary the strokes working across the scratches.

Wooden sticks wrapped with bonded emery paper are a convenient tool and are especially useful when sanding curves, corners and hard-to-reach areas. Emery sticks can be purchased in a variety of shapes including flat, round and half-round. However, these can be easily fabricated in the studio with small sticks such as coffee stirrers. Using double-sided tape, attach pieces of wet and dry paper to the sticks, covering all sides.

A pendant motor, mounted with a split mandrel, can be especially useful for sanding items with flat and curved surfaces, such as the inside of ring shanks or bangles. Cut strips of wet and dry paper of the appropriate grade and thread the end of the strip through the split mandrel. Proceed to wind the strip around the mandrel in the direction of rotation. As long as the paper strip has been wound in the correct direction, it will remain tightly wound as the motor turns.

Small sticks can be covered with wet and dry paper and used to sand hard-to-reach places.

As the piece is sanded, the paper's grit will wear away. Simply tear off the used portion to reveal unused layers of paper beneath.

When working on uncomplicated designs it is sensible to sand any imperfections in one go once all the soldering has been completed. However, when constructing an intricate and complex piece, it may be necessary to remove some excess solder before the soldering process is finished. If it will be difficult to access certain areas when the piece is completed, those areas should be smoothed during fabrication. If a test piece has been prepared, study it and decide what areas of the piece are less accessible.

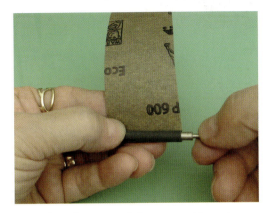

Threading the wet and dry paper strip onto a split mandrel.

JEWELLERY FINDINGS

Findings are essential elements of jewellery design as they help link the piece of jewellery to the body, making the design functional and wearable. Their role of joining together components makes them an important element when planning and making an item of jewellery. A well-designed finding will add security without detracting from the integrity of the piece. It can provide interesting detail to the overall design or can alternatively be unobtrusive and discreet.

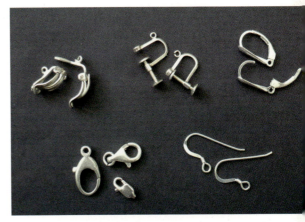

A collection of ready-made findings includes ear clips, continental ear wires, lobster clasp, trigger clasp, carabiner catch and ear wires.

COMMERCIALLY BOUGHT FINDINGS

Commercially produced jewellery findings are easy to source. Shops that sell jewellery-making materials offer a wide selection of styles in many varieties of metals and finishes. Using ready-made findings can save time as they can be incorporated unobtrusively into a bespoke design. Although certain items such as earring scrolls and posts provide a secure connection to the body, they have little visual impact so using commercially produced ones will not detract from the overall look of the piece. Other items such as lobster clasps, carabiner catches, ear clips and cufflink fittings have movable parts that would be time-consuming and difficult to produce, especially if the finding is small.

Findings such as ear wires or larger clasps are visually prominent and the overall design of the piece can benefit greatly from thoughtful incorporation. Designing and making the findings will be preferable to purchasing ready-made. Even small details can enhance the cohesiveness of the final design.

MAKING FINDINGS

Jump Rings

Jump rings are indispensable components used to join elements in jewellery designs. They can provide a secure connection as well as help lend movement and manoeuvrability. Chains are made using many jump rings linked together. Although jump rings can be sourced

To quickly produce a few jump rings, wind the wire around round-nose pliers while gripping the wire securely.

Wire wound around a wooden dowel or metal rod secured in a vice will produce jump rings of a consistent size.

Container of sorted jump rings.

prefabricated, they are easy to make in the studio in large quantities, at a very low cost.

To make a small quantity of jump rings quickly, simply wind the wire around a pair of round-nose pliers. Grasping the wire with the pliers and rotating the pliers so the wire spirals down toward the narrow end will produce jump rings of a fairly consistent size. Be careful not to pinch too tightly as this can leave marks in the wire.

To produce a number of jump rings of exactly the same size, it can be helpful to use a wooden dowel or a metal rod of the required diameter in a vice. Clamp the wire with the dowel or rod into the vice and wind the wire around it, keeping the coils tight.

Large quantities of jump rings are easily produced using a hand drill and a vice. Small batches of various sizes can be made and conveniently stored in small containers, readily available for use in future projects. Remember to use eye protection when working with the wire.

Step by Step: Making Jump Rings

1. Start by securing the drill in the vice. Choose a metal rod or wooden dowel of the required diameter around which to wind the wire.

2. Using fully annealed wire in the chosen gauge, tighten the rod or dowel together with the end of the wire in the jaws of the drill chuck.

3. Slowly start the drill with one hand, feeding the wire around the rod or dowel with the other hand, keeping the wire taut and the coils close together. Cut the wire once the desired number of rings has been coiled.

After winding the wire into a coil, the rings will need to be cut apart. Using flush cutters is not recommended because this will require an extra cut as the pinched side of each ring will need to be

Making jump rings – Step 1.

Step 2.

Step 3.

trimmed to make it flush. In addition, the resulting jump rings will not be uniform in size. The best alternative is to use an adjustable saw: this will provide a straight cut with two flush sides to the ends of the rings. If a wooden dowel is used, the wire can be cut directly on the dowel using the saw. If a metal rod has been used to form the wire, the coil must be removed before piercing.

Step by Step: Cutting the Coil of Wire

1. Slide the coil off the rod. Holding the coil against the bench peg for support, start to cut from the bottom, using the jeweller's saw. Continue cutting through the coil. The jump rings should fall off and slide down the blade, gathering at the bottom of the frame.

2. If the wire has been wound around a wooden dowel, the rings can be cut directly on the dowel.

Cutting the coil of wire – Step 1.

Step 2.

Opening and Closing Jump Rings

When using jump rings to assemble components, the rings must be opened and closed in the correct manner. Wire can be work-hardened by twisting and hammering, but too much stress can cause metal fatigue; this is a weakening of the metal caused by microscopic cracks. Opening jump rings in the correct way will help maintain strength by avoiding putting too much stress on the wire. The jump ring will also retain its round shape and remain free from unsightly dents.

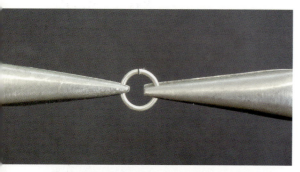

Opening and closing jump rings – Step 1.

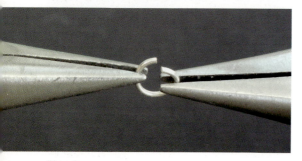

Step 2.

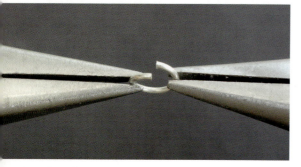

Step 3.

Step by Step: Opening and Closing Jump Rings

1. Use two pairs of snipe-nose pliers. Positioning the opening of the ring at the top, grip the jump-ring on both sides of the split with the two pairs of pliers.

2. Twist, moving one hand toward you and the other away, until the jump ring is open.

3. To close the jump ring, reverse this procedure. Grip the jump ring again with the two pairs of pliers, moving your hands in the opposite direction so the ends again line up. It can help to gently move the ends back and forth until you feel them meet. Ideally, the wires should mesh tightly, creating a perfect joint.

EAR WIRES

Earrings hanging from an ear wire have a sense of movement. Aside from functioning as a connection to the body, ear wires can add interest and can be designed in harmony with their dangling component. They are easy to make and their length and size can be tailored to suit a specific design. Most ear wires are made using 0.8 or 0.9mm round wire. Finer wire tends not to be robust enough and heavier wire can be too thick to use in most piercings.

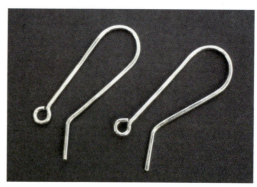

Ear wires.

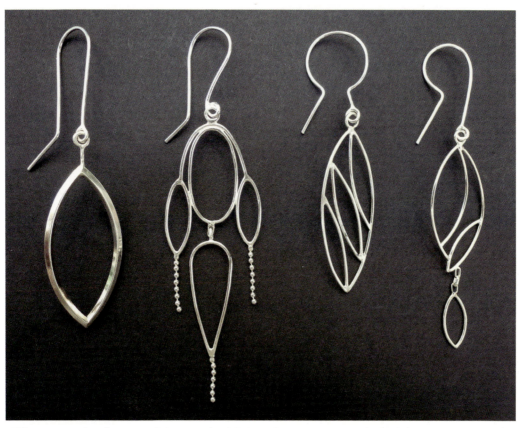

Different ear wire shapes and sizes can be fabricated to create a specific look for the overall earring design.

Sketching alternatives not only helps you decide on a specific design, but also informs you about the amount of wire needed for the pair of ear wires. Measure the length of the ear wire in your sketch, making sure to add enough wire for both the bend at the top and the loop at the bottom. Using copper wire as a test piece can be helpful. The following instructions are a guide for making one style of ear wire. Changing the angles, curves and length of wire will enable you to create a variety of styles to suit your designs.

Step by Step: Making a Pair of Ear Wires

1. Using flush cutters, cut two lengths of 0.8mm wire, each 6cm long.

Making a pair of ear wires – Step 1.

2. Using flat- or snipe-nose pliers, make a shallow bend in the wire about 8mm from the end: this short bend will create the loop.

3. Grasp the end of the wire with the round-nose pliers. Make a loop, taking care that the end of the wire meets cleanly, as you may choose to solder it.

4. Bend the wire around a small mandrel. Choose the area of the mandrel to correspond to the size of the bend you would like to make.

5. File or paper the end of the wire, carefully making sure that it is smooth and will be comfortable to wear.

Making a pair of ear wires – Step 2.

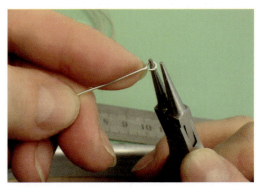

Step 3.

Step 4.

Step 5.

Step 6.

Step 7.

6. Using snipe-nose pliers, make a shallow curve in the wire about 8mm from the tip.

7. Harden the ear wire by using the flat end of a planishing or repoussé hammer. Gently hammer the wire on the bench block. The wire will flatten slightly at it is hammered but this will help the wire to keep its shape. Avoid hammering the small loop, as this will need to be opened during assembly. Soldering the ear wire closed after the components have been assembled is recommended. If you do so, harden it after it has been soldered.

CLASPS

Most necklaces, especially those that are worn short around the neck, require a clasp. An ornate clasp can embellish a neckpiece and can be a focal point in the design. Alternatively, a clasp can also be designed to be unobtrusive so that it is barely visible and is subtly integrated with the other elements of the piece. A hook and ring clasp is functional and discreet. Choosing to use different gauges and shapes of wire as well as adapting the ring's form can provide endless variations on the basic hook and ring clasp design. All elements of a clasp should be soldered, as it is important that the catch is secure.

Step by Step: Making a Basic Hook and Ring Clasp

1. Cut a 4.5cm length of 1.2mm round wire. Make sure that both ends are flush.

2. Using flat-or snipe-nose pliers, make a shallow bend in the wire about 13mm from the end: this short bend will create the loop.

The discreet hook and ring clasp on this neckpiece is barely visible when worn.

A simple hook attaches to a component which functions as the ring.

Basic hook and ring clasp.

Making a pair of ear wires – Step 1.

Step 2.

Step 3.

Step 4.

Step 5.

Step 6.

Step 7.

3. Holding the wire at the bend using flat-nose pliers, grasp the end of the wire with the round-nose pliers. Make a loop taking care that the end of the wire meets cleanly.

4. File and paper the end to make it smooth.

5. Bend the wire around a small mandrel to create the hook.

Step 8.

6. Using half-round-nose pliers, make a shallow curve at the end of the wire.

7. Apply a small amount of easy solder paste. Solder, quench and pickle. File or paper away any excess solder.

8. Attach the hook to the end of the chain. Solder the chain link, quench and pickle. File or paper away any excess solder.

9. Place the hook on the bench block and gently hammer to work-harden the wire.

Step 9.

INCORPORATING COMMERCIALLY PRODUCED FINDINGS

On occasion, a design requires a clasp or other attachment that is small and secure. Delicate catches and findings with movable parts can be time-consuming to design and fabricate, and in some cases, a commercially made finding can be superior to one produced in the studio. The key is sourcing a finding that complements the piece, providing security or movement without sacrificing the cohesiveness of the design.

Findings with movable parts, such as certain cufflink fittings, are ideal commercially produced items to integrate into your designs. Prepare to solder the findings by carefully setting up the item to be joined on a fireproof brick using a third hand to help position the components. As the piece will not need to be reheated after the incorporation of the finding, use easy solder, applying the paste sparingly. Solder with caution, keeping the flame concentrated on the soldered joint so as not to damage the spring. After soldering, remove any excess solder using needle files and wet and dry paper. The piece can be tumbled in the barrel polisher.

Making a chain to complement a pendant can be time-consuming, yet satisfying (*see* Chapter 6 for instructions for making chain). However, if a simple or delicate chain is required, it is easy to purchase finished chain, ready-made with the clasp attached. A third alternative is to purchase and assemble loose chain with an appropriate clasp. This provides greater flexibility regarding the choice of the length and style of the chain as well as the style and size of clasp.

Commercially produced earring posts and scrolls are made in sterling silver, 9ct gold and 18ct gold. The posts can be found in various lengths and the scrolls in assorted sizes and styles. Soldering the posts to earring components is easy to do.

Commercially produced cufflink fittings can be easily integrated into a design.

A length of chain is carefully soldered to a commercially produced clasp.

Soldering earring posts – Step 1.

Step 2.

Step by Step: Soldering Earring Posts

1. Place the earring components on a fireproof brick. Using a third hand, set the posts in place and apply easy solder sparingly.

2. As the post will be smaller than the earring component, be careful not to direct the flame onto the post as it can easily melt. Instead, concentrate the flame in the juncture to be soldered.

3. After pickling and sanding away any imperfections, straighten the post if necessary and give it a twist or two: this will work-harden the wire and make it stiff.

Step 3.

CHAIN MAKING

Making chain can be a time-consuming task. However, a hand-made chain will be a unique piece, reflecting the individuality of the maker and unlike anything produced by a machine. Many makers enjoy the long process of chain fabrication and feel that the finished chain is well worth the investment of time and patience.

When designing a chain, it is best to first consider its intended function. Will it be used to hang a large pendant? If so, it must be robust enough to support the weight of the pendant. A chain that is intended to be worn on its own can be of a more fragile design. What will the length of the finished chain be? A long chain will not necessarily require a clasp if it can easily fit over the head of the wearer, but a clasp can make the design more versatile by allowing the chain to be worn in a single or double loop. A shorter chain will require a clasp and decisions must be made regarding the clasp itself. The clasp can be discreetly integrated into the chain or can be designed as a prominent feature of the piece. Will the chain be comprised of similar links or will they vary in shape and size? If using links of varied size and weight the balance of the chain can be affected and it may be necessary to ensure that the piece hangs well.

The look and feel of a chain can be altered by choosing between a variety of elements. Besides making decisions on the gauge of the wire and the size and shape of the links, a chain can be made more individual and unique by:

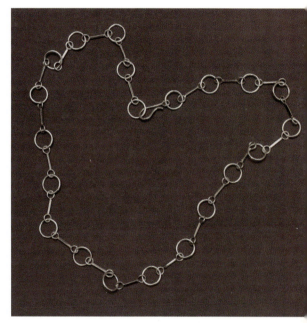

Variation of the wire shape and size adds interest to this heavy chain.

- texturing the wire by hammering
- stretching or manipulating the links with pliers
- combining different shapes of wire
- combining varied gauges of the wire
- using twisted or patterned wire
- incorporating decorative elements.

Exploring these alternatives by making test sections of chain can be a good way to help commit to a design before producing and assembling a large number of links. The following instructions present a few tips and techniques used to produce two, quite contrasting, styles of chain. In both examples, the chains are made as secure as possible by soldering each link. As the jump rings will not need to be soldered more than once, easy solder can be used.

This first chain is made using wire of different shapes and gauges. The round jump rings are fabricated using round wire. Interspersed between these are component pieces made from square wire with small jump rings soldered on each end. Begin by deciding on the approximate length of the chain you plan to make and calculate the number of jump rings and component pieces that will be required to complete it. In this case, a section of 9 jump rings and 9 components measures just about 20 cm in length. Fabricating the amount needed from the start is not essential but will save time.

Step by Step: Making a Chain combining Round and Square Wire

1. Start by making jump rings using fully annealed 1mm round wire. The circumference of these rings is approximately 1cm. Do not solder the jump rings closed.

2. Take a length of 1.2mm square wire and, using a bench block and leather mallet, hammer the wire to remove any bend or curve.

3. Cut small lengths measuring 8mm. Using flush cutters will slightly pinch the wire's square profile, but this should not be a problem, as the ends will be soldered to the smaller jump rings. The backside of the flush cutters will leave a distorted end that will need to be trimmed with each cut.

Making a chain combining round and square wire – Step 1.

Step 2.

Step 3.

Step 4.

Step 5.

Step 6.

Step 7.

Step 8.

4. Using fully annealed 0.9mm round wire, make the smaller jump rings that will be soldered on the ends of the square lengths. These small rings have a circumference of approximately 4mm.

5. Set out a group of square wire lengths on a fireproof brick. Position the small jump rings at the ends with the joints meeting the square lengths. Apply easy solder paste and solder, concentrating the flame on the joints.

6. Pickle and file or paper any excess solder. Check that all the joints are strong.

7. Open the larger jump rings and thread the component pieces on. Close the rings, taking care that the ends mesh perfectly.

8. Place on a fireproof brick and apply solder paste, taking care to keep the attached component away from the area to be soldered. Solder, concentrating the flame on the joints.

Step 9.

9. Repeat the process until all the links are attached. Test each link to be sure that the solder joint is strong. Re-solder any joints that have not been properly connected. Pickle and file or paper any excess solder.

10. Tumble the chain in the barrel polisher. This will work-harden and polish the chain. Finish the chain as desired (*see* Chapter 8).

Step 10.

Our second chain is made from 0.8mm round wire. Each link is made from a 3cm length of wire and each finished hexagon measures approximately 1cm across. Pliers are used to form the hexagonal shape but other angular shapes such as triangles and squares can be made using the same technique. The marks left by the pliers help to lend a look of fragility to the chain. But as each link is properly soldered, and the chain work hardened, it is more robust than it appears. Using 0.9mm round wire will produce a chain that is slightly heavier but the look and feel will be different.

CREATING OVAL JUMP RINGS

Jump rings can be fabricated in a variety of shapes to change the appearance of a chain. Oval jump rings, for example, can be quickly fabricated from round ones. Using a soldered jump ring that has not been work-hardened, place it over the jaws of a pair of round-nose pliers. Pulling the pliers gently apart will stretch the ring into an oval shape.

Oval jump rings are easy to form using pliers.

Step by Step: Making Chain using Round Wire

1. Start by making jump rings using annealed round wire (*see* Chapter 5). As each ring is fabricated using a 3cm length of wire, choose a dowel with the diameter of 9.5mm. The rings will be manipulated with pliers later on, so they need not have a perfectly round shape at this stage.

2. Take approximately half of the jump rings and check that all of the joints mesh perfectly. Solder them on a fireproof brick, working in small batches to save time. There is no need to pickle at this stage.

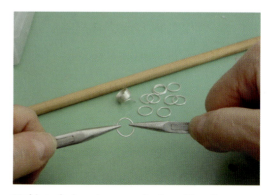

Making chain using round wire – Step 1.

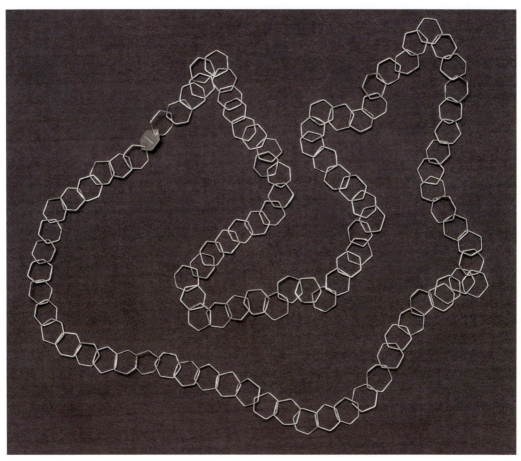

This delicate chain is made of 100 hexagonal links.

3. Using the unsoldered jump rings, join a number of links together making short lengths that will fit comfortably on the fire-proof brick. Position the new joints in a way that they will be most accessible by the flame. Apply solder sparingly.

Step 2.

Step 3.

Step 4.

Step 5.

Step 6.

Step 7.

Step 8.

4. Solder the series of interconnected links, concentrating the flame on the new joints. There is no need to pickle at this stage. Test each link to be sure that the solder joint is strong. Re-solder any joints that have not been properly connected.

5. Repeat until the links have been soldered into workable lengths. Now, using a new jump ring, join each length with the next, keeping the flame away from the finished lengths. Test the new joints and then pickle the entire length of rough chain.

6. Each link will now need to be formed. Using snipe-nose pliers, flatten each facet of the jump ring by squeezing tightly with the pliers.

7. After the links have been formed to the desired shape, they may not be perfectly flat. To flatten the links, place them individually on the bench block and gently hammer with a rawhide mallet.

8. File or sand any excess solder. Tumble the chain in the barrel polisher. This will work harden and polish the chain. Finish the chain as desired (*see* Chapter 8).

MANIPULATING JUMP RINGS INTO ANGULAR SHAPES

To create an angular jump ring, use a soldered jump ring that has not been work-hardened. Using snipe-nose pliers, tightly squeeze the wire to produce a flat area. The shape of the ring will depend on the number of flattened facets and their width. Making test pieces using copper wire will help to master this technique. Be aware that both silver and gold will be more difficult to manipulate, as they are not as soft as copper when annealed.

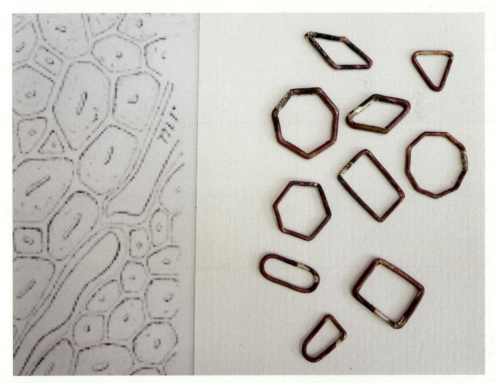

Making test pieces will help guide the choice of the width of each facet.

CONSTRUCTING STRUCTURAL SHAPES

Wire can be manipulated and soldered to create jewellery that is light and easy to wear on the body. Because it is lightweight, wire can be used successfully to construct larger pieces of jewellery. Once basic soldering skills have been mastered, it may be interesting to progress to using wire to create more complicated structural forms. A variety of exciting designs can be created using basic wire-working processes combined with good planning and patience.

PREPARATION

Constructing structural shapes requires a good deal of planning. Start by reflecting on what type of piece you are interested in making. A ring, bracelet, pendant, earring or brooch will each have different features that need to be taken into account. Designing jewellery that is easy to wear involves making practical considerations regarding size and weight. In order for a piece to function properly, it must be both light enough and strong enough. The robustness of the piece must be compatible with its function so factoring in the gauge of wire is an important detail to consider, especially as finer gauges of wire will not be strong enough for hard-wearing items such as rings and bangles.

Evaluate the form of the piece and be satisfied that the shape and size work well in how it relates to the body.

CONSTRUCTING A FORM

Building a flat-sided form combined with a structural aspect can be a good beginning project. Structures of this type can be used, for example, to make earrings and cufflinks as the flat side is easy to solder onto an earring stud or cufflink fitting. A cufflink must be robust enough to be worn on a cuff where it may be subjected to daily knocks and scratches, so choosing a larger gauge of wire provides strength and stability.

After making preliminary sketches, refine a sketch to include specific details regarding the dimensions of the piece. Making a test piece at this

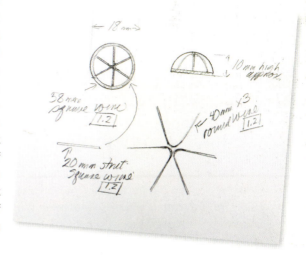

Sketches can include estimates of the wire's shape, length and gauge to help determine the amount that will be necessary for fabrication of the piece.

These cufflink components are made using both round and square wire.

stage will provide you with more information, such as specific wire lengths for the structural part of the piece. The following instructions are for a single component made with 1.2mm round and square wire. The circular base measures approximately 2cm in width.

Step by Step:
Constructing a Structural Shape

1. Using annealed square 1.2mm wire, cut a length measuring 57mm to make the circular base. Use flush cutters and be sure to make the ends of the wire flat by filing. Use half-round pliers to form into a ring.

2. Solder the ring using hard or medium solder. Pickle and make round using a mandrel, then hammer flat using a rawhide mallet.

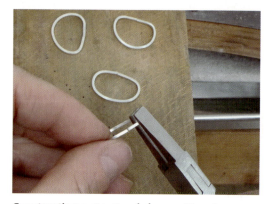

Constructing a structural shape – Step 1.

3. Cut an 18mm length of square wire for the strut. Adjust the length of wire using a needle file, filing carefully so the strut fits precisely across the centre of the ring. Solder using hard or medium solder. Pickle and then confirm that the component lies flat, using a rawhide mallet if necessary.

Step 2.

Step 3.

Step 4.

Step 5.

Step 6.

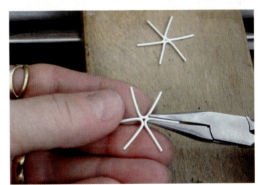

Step 7.

4. Using annealed round 1.2mm wire, cut three 28mm lengths. These will need to be soldered together to form the top of the dome shaped structure.

5. Taking round-nose pliers, make a V-shaped bend at the centre of all three lengths.

6. Set up the lengths on a fireproof brick so that the curves meet in the middle with the wires radiating outward, evenly interspersed. Solder the juncture using a very small amount of hard or medium solder and pickle the piece.

7. Using snipe-nose pliers, manipulate the six wire ends so they fan out in an even pattern.

8. Choose a doming punch in an appropriate size and secure it into the vice. Taking a rawhide mallet, tap the component gently onto the punch, forming a domed shape.

9. Using snipe-nose pliers, manipulate the six wire ends so they are evenly spaced, adjusting any awkward bends created during the doming process.

Step 8.

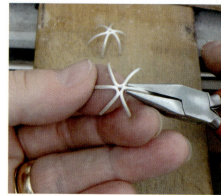

Step 9.

Step 10.

Step 11.

Step 12.

Step 13.

10. The six wire ends will now need to be adjusted and trimmed so they fit perfectly onto the ring component. Placing the domed wires on a flat surface can help ascertain which wires will need to be shortened. Trim and file the wires so they are flush with the ring.

11. When you are satisfied with the connection between the components, it is time to solder. Set up the two components on a fireproof block and add easy solder to one of the six wire ends. A third hand can be used to steady the domed component.

12. Quench the piece and reposition the remaining five wire ends so they meet the ring component perfectly. File the longer ends if necessary. Concentrate the flame at the solder joints and solder the five connections. Quench, pickle and check that all the joints are secure.

13. File away any excess solder and sand smooth with wet and dry paper. Add any connection or finding to the piece using easy solder. Tumble in a barrel polisher and finish as desired (see Chapter 8).

CONSTRUCTING A TWO-SIDED FORM

Designing two-sided wire structures can be an enjoyable challenge. As the pieces can be viewed from different angles and from the top through to the bottom, details can be designed to either mirror or complement the reverse side. Choosing a finer gauge of wire when designing a pendant, earring or brooch is reasonable as the risk of damage during wear is quite low. Constructing the piece using fine wire adds a feel of delicacy which, fortunately, can be quite deceiving. The construction, once work-hardened in a barrel polisher, will be much stronger than it appears. Designing a piece with too few wire struts can create a weaker structure as the wire struts help provide strength. Sketching followed by making test pieces is the best way to decide upon a final design. Experiment with different gauges of wire.

Sketch a number of options for the construction of the design. If aiming to create two different patterns to complement each other, layering

Using tracing paper to see two sketched layers together can help inform design decisions.

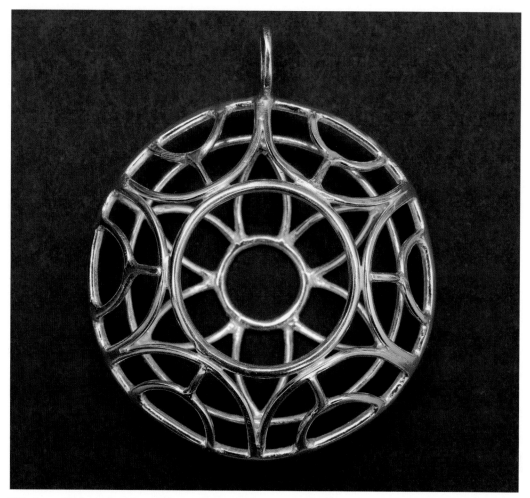

This two-sided pendant has different linear designs on each side.

the sketches over each other can be helpful to see how the two sides will work together. After sketching various alternatives for the bottom of the piece, use tracing paper and draw a selection for the top. The sketches made on the tracing paper can then be viewed in alternative combinations with the original drawing.

When constructing a two-sided form using many wire connections, the biggest challenge involves the set-up and positioning of the different elements for soldering. Secure set-up can be achieved using a variety of methods, and with increased practice you will find which method best suits your way of working. I tend to rely on

the use of third hands to hold and support the wires as they are positioned on fireproof bricks. Experimenting with alternative techniques as you progress will help you find the ones that you personally find most suitable.

The following example is a two-sided form which is circular in shape and constructed using 1.2mm and 0.8mm round wire. The heavier wire is used on the outer edge and most of the other circular shapes in the design. The finer 0.8mm wire is used to create the geometric patterns. The piece measures approximately 35mm across and is 15mm deep. This type of design builds upon the skills learned from the previous example.

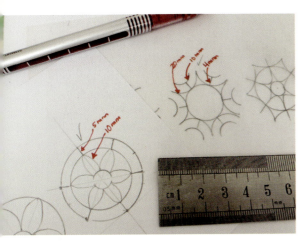

Constructing a two-sided form – Step 1.

Step 2.

Step by Step: Constructing a Two-Sided Form

1. After committing to a design, note the length of each wire that will be required. When estimating the lengths of the wires needed for the two domed sides of the design, add a few millimetres to each wire's length. The excess is necessary, as the wires will need to be trimmed as you progress with the fabrication and the joining of the two sides.

Step 3.

2. Start by fabricating the circular elements of the design using medium or hard solder. Use a rawhide mallet to make the components flat. There is no need to file or sand the rings at this point.

3. Use a mandrel to form any curved wires needed for the design. The wires can be manipulated after soldering but will retain a cleaner shape if formed in the correct shape from the start.

4. Cut the individual wires needed for the piece. Use a rawhide mallet to flatten them if necessary. All wires require precise measurement but as you will be trimming the wires as you progress with soldering, there is no need for the ends to be cut flush.

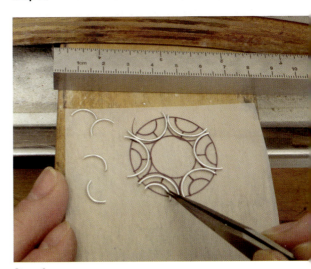

Step 4.

5. Marking out with permanent marker can help to accurately line up the wires before soldering.

6. Beginning with the wires that form the base of the design, carefully position them on a fireproof brick.

7. Solder the innermost joints using medium or hard solder. Quench and pickle.

8. Before soldering new elements onto the design, prepare the ends of the attaching wires. Trim them to the required length and make flush.

9. Continue to add elements, soldering with medium or hard solder, until the side of the piece is completely soldered. With consecutive applications of heat, try to focus the flame on the new joints.

10. Choose a large doming punch and secure it in the vice. Taking a rawhide mallet, tap the component gently onto the punch, forming a shallow domed shape. Alternatively, the wires can be formed using half-round pliers.

11. Use pliers to adjust the wires, refining the pattern. Any reshaping will need to be done at this stage as it often cannot be done successfully after soldering to the outer ring. Use snipe-nose pliers to straighten and half-round-nose pliers to improve curves.

12. Test the fit of the component to the outer ring and trim or file the ends of the wires so that they are the correct length. Placing the component on a flat surface will help determine that all contact points lie flush.

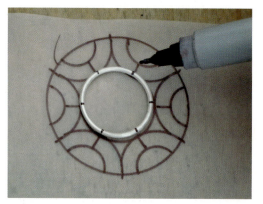

Step 5.

Step 6.

Step 7.

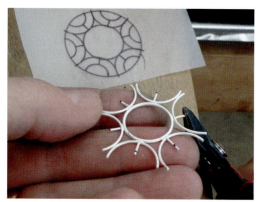

Step 8.

Step 9.

Step 10.

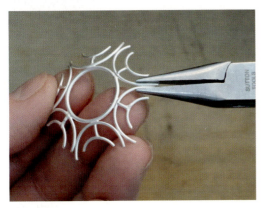

Step 11.

Step 12.

Step 13.

Step 14.

13. Use dividers to confirm the correct lengths of the wires, especially if symmetry is a key element of the design.

14. Place the component on the ring and solder one or two joints using easy solder. Use a third hand to steady the pieces if necessary. Check your progress and adjust and file any wires that are not flush. Replace the piece on the soldering

block, add easy solder and continue soldering the junctures. Check that all the joints have been soldered, quench, pickle and set the piece aside.

15. Fabricate the second side of the piece using steps 5 to 11.

16. Once any adjustments have been completed, trim the outer wires in preparation to join the two halves together.

17. At this stage, use needle files and wet and dry paper to remove any excess solder from the concave sides of the two components. These areas will be difficult to access when the pieces have been soldered together.

18. Fit the two sides together and mark out any wires that need to be trimmed for a good connection. Using flush cutters, trim at the correct angle. Use needle files to adjust the wire ends if necessary.

Step 15.

Step 16.

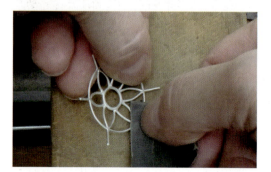

Step 17.

Step 18.

Step 19.

Step 20.

19. Once you are satisfied with the connection between the components, set them on the fireproof brick for soldering. A third hand can be used to assist in stabilizing the contact. Start by soldering one or two base wires using easy solder. This will allow for any necessary manipulation of the remaining wires during the soldering process. Continue until all the joints have been soldered. Quench and pickle.

20. If the piece is a pendant or earring, add any connection for hanging at this time using easy solder. Using needle files, remove any excess solder from the piece. Sand with wet and dry paper and tumble the piece in a barrel polisher. Finish as desired.

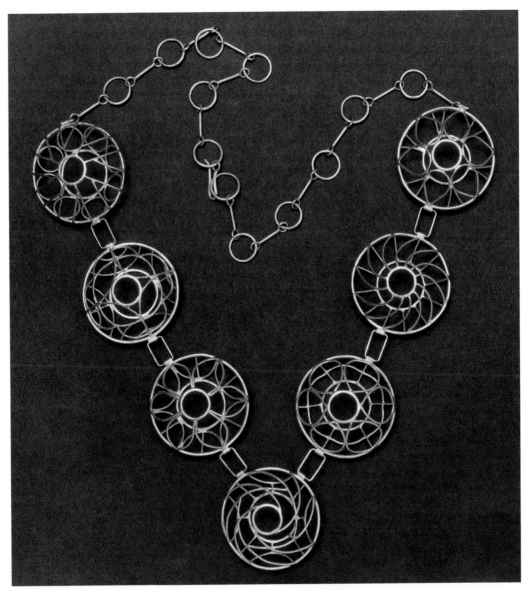

This necklace is composed of seven components, each with a different design.

SURFACE FINISHES

A good-quality finish is an important aspect of a jewellery design and can greatly enhance the overall look of the piece. Once an item of jewellery has been filed and sanded smooth using a fine grade of wet and dry paper, it is time to give it a polished, matt, satin or oxidized finish. It is important that you are satisfied with the surface quality of the piece before starting to apply the finish. A beautifully rendered finish will often complement the overall design but cannot be used to hide imperfect filing and sanding. The finishing process may be a time-consuming task but the result is often worth the effort.

HIGHLY POLISHED FINISHES

Many jewellers use polishing motors to help them achieve a highly polished finish to their work. These machines are perfect for providing a superior finish on larger items of jewellery. Polishing compounds, such as tripoli or rouge, are applied to large circular mops attached to the machine that rapidly spins them. The item of jewellery is held securely and gently pushed against the rotating mops, and the metal's surface is buffed as tiny scratches are removed. Polishing motors are not suitable for chain and other small and intricate items of jewellery. Using small mops and brushes attached to a pendant motor or a barrel polisher is a better alternative.

Polishing using Pendant Motor

Attach a small polishing mop to a pendant motor and start by using tripoli, a coarser grade of polishing compound. Follow with a second polishing using rouge to create a highly polished surface. The friction produced during polishing may cause the item of jewellery to become very warm. If it becomes too hot to handle, put it down and wait a few seconds before continuing to polish.

Care must be taken when using a pendant motor for polishing. Always wear goggles and a dust mask and tie back long hair. Polishing can be a quite a dirty job and small particles will be produced during the process. The goggles will protect against any items that may be flung from the pendant motor due to the polisher's incorrect grip. After polishing a piece of jewellery,

Rouge applied on a small felt brush can help give a highly polished finish.

Radial abrasive discs are ideal tools to help polish delicate pieces.

Stainless steel shot is mixed with water and barrelling compound.

USING A BARREL POLISHER

A barrel polisher is an essential tool for polishing small items and chains. It work-hardens the pieces as it polishes. A number of pieces can be placed in the polisher together although chains should be tumbled alone to prevent tangling.

Place the shot in the drum together with a small amount of barrelling compound and enough water to cover the shot. Use the recommended amount of compound; a teaspoon or two should be enough depending on the size of the barrel. Aside from lubricating the components, the compound helps keep the shot in good condition by preventing rust.

MATT AND SATIN FINISHES

An alternative to a highly polished finish can be achieved in different ways. A range of materials can impart various textures ranging from a flat matt to a lustrous satin appearance. Making test pieces using combinations of the following materials will help you find the best finish to suit your design.

gently clean away any residue using an ultrasonic cleaner or water and washing-up liquid on a soft toothbrush.

Radial abrasive disks are used to help remove scratches and polish hard-to-reach areas. These small flexible disks, available in a range of grades, are mounted on the pendant motor. They help provide a clean and effective way of working on smaller, delicate jewellery items without the application of rouge.

This Line and Form See Saw Ring by Catherine Hendy has a lustrous matt finish.

Materials for Finishing

- Washing-up liquid: most household dishwashing detergents will work well.
- Liquid abrasive cleaner: a basic household cleaning product also known as Cif contains a fine grit.
- Toothbrush.
- Pumice powder: this fine abrasive powder available from jewellery tool suppliers can be mixed with water and washing-up liquid to create a paste. Applying the paste with a toothbrush will create a soft satin finish: if a little more brightness is desired, follow by brushing with liquid abrasive cleaner.
- Brass brush: a fine-bristled brush available from jewellery tool suppliers can be used to create a brushed matt finish on metal. In order to prevent brass particles from embedding on the metal surface, it should be used together with washing-up liquid and water.
- Steel wire wool: this can be sourced in various coarseness grades and can be used to create a matt or satin finish. A fine grade of wool used with washing-up liquid will create a brighter finish.
- Scouring pads: these household cleaning pads are made of a green synthetic material and can be used dry or with water and washing-up liquid to create a matt finish.
- Abrasive rubber block: available from jewellery tool suppliers, this is impregnated with abrasive grit and can be sourced in various coarseness grades. It can be cut to the required size and shape and used to clean metal or create a satin finish. One well-known brand is Garryflex.

Pumice powder, steel wire wool and scouring pads are products used to impart matt and satin finishes to metal jewellery.

Pumice paste is applied with a toothbrush to enable access to hard-to-reach areas.

OXIDIZING SILVER

Oxidation is a natural process that causes metal to tarnish. The application of an oxidizing solution will greatly speed this process and create a black or dark grey patina on sterling silver. The patination lies on the surface and, because of this, does not damage the metal. A designer may choose to oxidize the entire item of jewellery or only particular areas to create contrast or to highlight details of a design. Oxidation can produce stunning results but will work only on silver, copper and brass, not on gold.

The oxidized patina on this sterling silver cuff accentuates the graphic leaf shapes.

When using oxidizing chemicals, it is vital to follow the manufacturer's instructions and work in a well-ventilated area. Always wear gloves and an apron for protection. The surface of the metal must be clean and free from oils and grease that can prevent good contact between the oxidizing solution and the metal. To be confident that the metal is clean, prepare it by using pumice powder mixed with water. Using a toothbrush, clean the piece with the pumice paste; rinse and leave to dry before proceeding with oxidizing.

As with other finishing processes, patination should be done at the end of fabrication. It is important to be aware that the jewellery's oxidized finish will rub away with normal use, especially on pieces that are subject to more wear. A coating of beeswax polish to the surface of the piece will offer some protection. If you are not happy with the oxidation, it can be removed by annealing and pickling.

Materials for Creating an Oxidized Finish

- Oxidizing solution such as liver of sulphur (ammonium hydro-sulphide). Liver of sulphur can be purchased in liquid and crystal form and is available from jewellery tool suppliers. The liquid will need to be diluted with water before use. It produces an oxidized patina on silver and copper. Other oxidizing solutions are manufactured which are used in slightly different ways. Platinol, for example, is applied without mixing with water. It can be brushed on or the jewellery piece can be immersed in the full-strength liquid.
- Plastic tweezers.
- Small ceramic or glass bowl.
- Disposable latex gloves.
- Apron.
- Beeswax polish: this can be applied to an oxidized piece of jewellery to help protect the patina.

Step by Step: Oxidizing using Liquid Liver of Sulphur

1. Clean the item of jewellery using pumice paste and a toothbrush. Wearing rubber gloves will help keep the piece grease-free. Rinse well and leave to dry.

Step 1.

2. Prepare the liver of sulphur solution according to the manufacturer's instructions. The mixture cannot be stored and reused, so mix only enough for the project at hand.

Step 2.

3. Place the piece into the solution. It should not require more than a minute to change to a black colour. When the colour is dark enough, remove with plastic tweezers and rinse thoroughly with cold tap water.

Step 3.

BURNISHING

If a matt or satin finish has been used on a piece, the edges can be burnished to highlight the shape and give a contrasting surface texture.

PLATING

Electroplating is a process used to introduce a fine layer of metal to the surface of metal jewellery. A layer of plate is measured in microns, which is a very fine layer (1 micron = 0.001mm). The thicker the plate on a piece of jewellery, the longer it will last when worn. Rings, earrings, necklaces and brooches can require varying thickness of plate to ensure long wear. For instance, a ring will be subjected to harder wear then a necklace, which receives less handling when worn. If choosing to plate an item, it is important to be aware that the finish may not last in the long term. Fortunately, the piece can be re-plated if the layer starts to wear away. Also, any repair or alteration to the piece that requires soldering will damage the plate, and the plating process will need to be repeated.

Plating with 24ct gold will give the piece a warm, rich colour.

Gold Plating

Gold plating is commonly used on items of silver jewellery. Sterling silver plated with gold can have the appearance of the more precious metal but at a fraction of the cost. Used as a decorative effect, elements of a design can be plated, leaving areas of silver as a contrasting colour. Yellow gold plate can be done in 9ct to 24ct with the higher carat gold having the most brilliant colour. Gold plating can also be done in other colours including white, rose and green gold.

Choosing the number of microns of gold plating to use will make a difference in the cost of the process. Flash plating, equal to 0.175 microns, is inexpensive but far too thin to be used on jewellery. The minimum thickness for gold electroplating is 0.5 microns although using a heavier plate, between 1 and 5 microns, is advisable.

'Vermeil' refers to sterling silver that has been plated with a minimum of 2.5 microns of gold. Labelling an item of jewellery as vermeil helps to assure the buyer of the quality of the gold plate.

Rhodium Plating

Rhodium is frequently used in the jewellery industry to plate white gold, platinum and silver to give it a durable and brilliant white shiny surface. Platinum and palladium (a less expensive alternative to platinum) are used in much the same way. Interestingly, rhodium plating also can be done in black and blue colours. The colour of black rhodium is a dark grey-black, not dissimilar to an oxidized finish. It is long-wearing and can be applied to any precious metal, as compared to an oxidized finish, which can only be used on sterling silver. Blue rhodium is similar to black, but with a brighter blue colour.

USING PLATING AS A DECORATIVE ELEMENT

To achieve this two-toned effect, a special lacquer is applied to the finished sterling silver piece to prevent the gold from adhering to the surface of the metal during plating. Using a fine paintbrush, apply two layers of stopping-off lacquer, also known as Lacomit, to the area that is to retain the silver colour. The item is then plated in the normal manner. Subsequently the lacquer is removed and the piece cleaned.

Catherine Hendy uses plating as a decorative element to great effect in this set of Contrast Square Wire Rings.

CLEANING AND STORING JEWELLERY

Certain metals, particularly silver, will tarnish over time as they are exposed to air. The easiest way to help prevent this is to store silver pieces in airtight containers. Storing the jewellery together with anti-tarnish strips is also helpful: these paper strips are treated with an agent that absorbs moisture and airborne pollutants that cause the metal to tarnish.

Silver polishing cloths are a convenient and safe way to remove tarnish. Rubbing the jewellery with one of these soft cotton cloths (impregnated with a cleaning and anti-tarnishing agent) gently removes tarnish and brings back the shine to highly polished items. These polishing cloths are excellent for use on highly polished finishes but are not as suitable for jewellery with a matt or satin finish. Gold does not tarnish as readily as silver but if the jewellery item is made of a lower carat gold, particularly 9ct, some tarnishing will occur. Gold polishing cloths work in the same way as the silver cloths to remove the tarnish, leaving a highly polished finish.

Silver dip is a good option for removing tarnish on chain and delicate silver items especially if they have areas that are hard to reach with a polishing cloth. To use, simply dip the silver pieces into the liquid. A few seconds is often enough. It is advisable to keep the jewellery in contact with the silver dip for the shortest amount of time necessary since the chemical can damage the silver with excessive use. After removing the item from the dip, always rinse thoroughly under running water to clean away any traces of the chemicals. Dry with a soft cloth to avoid water marks.

To retain a good finish on gold-plated jewellery, treat the item with care during its use. To help protect and prolong the lifespan of the gold plating, avoid contact with perfumes and moisturizers and do not wear the jewellery while swimming or showering.

Silver dip removes tarnish from silver jewellery.

EMBELLISHMENTS AND DECORATIVE ELEMENTS

Gems, beads or pearls can be incorporated into a piece of wire jewellery as a way of embellishing and enhancing the design. These elements can be the focal point or a small accent on the design's structural form. Integrating gemstones or other materials can add a colourful detail to the otherwise monochrome shades of a silver or gold wire. Beads in either vibrant or subdued tones will also add a contrasting texture to hand-fabricated chain. Kinetic (moving) elements integrated into a piece can enhance interest and add a playful element to the design.

Embellishments should be added at the end of the making process. The heat from a torch, the harsh chemicals in a pickle and the rough tumbling of a barrel polisher will ruin most decorative elements. Using settings and cold connections, to join components of jewellery without heat, enables the jeweller to add precious and delicate ornamentation in a thoughtful and secure manner.

Beads in a variety of sizes and materials provide endless options for adding colour and texture to a necklace or bracelet.

INCORPORATING BEADS TO ACCENT A CHAIN

Adding beads in a chain can be an exciting way to introduce colour, texture and interesting shapes in a design. Beads can be made of an endless variety of materials; glass, semi-precious gems or pearl to name a few. Attaching beads with twisted wire is a good way to integrate them into the chain's design. Since no heat will be applied during the beading process, the decorative details can be made of an array of materials including resin, plastic, wood or paper.

When choosing beads to work with, there are two important considerations: the weight of the beads and the size of their holes. Carefully choose beads by checking the size of the holes in the beads on the strand. Although they may appear identical, on closer examination you may find that some beads have holes drilled in varying sizes. Some less expensive gemstone beads can be found with quite inconsistently sized holes, which can render a number of beads on a strand unfit for the intended beading project. The gauge of wire you intend to use to connect each bead to the other links will determine what hole size is required. Some softer beads, such as pearls, with small or irregular holes, can be drilled in the studio using special drill bits. However, it is much more difficult to adjust the size of a bead's hole when it is made from harder materials. Using fully annealed round wire of a diameter of 0.6 or 0.7mm is recommended for use in beading. If the beading wire is too fine, especially if the chain is long and heavy, the connection between the bead and the chain will be weak and the chain will not be durable enough for secure wear.

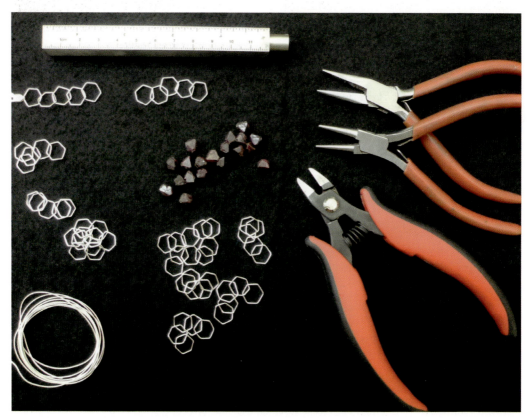

The chain's links and clasp are fabricated and finished before being joined to the beads.

This necklace is made of short lengths of chain interspersed with spinel beads.

When choosing the gauge of wire to use for the links, consider the chain's total length and weight as well as the weight of the beads themselves. The gauge of wire you use to fabricate the chain elements must be robust enough to bear the weight of the beads, but not too heavy for the beaded connections. The beads need to be distributed so that the chain hangs in a fluid manner, therefore thought should be given to their weight and placement.

Decide if the necklace or bracelet will include one or multiple beads. Make a sketch followed perhaps by a test piece using twine or string to help to decide on the number of beads to include and the length of the final piece. Determine if the design will include beads placed at regular intervals, or asymmetrically. When designing a necklace that includes asymmetrically spaced beads, a bit more planning may be necessary to achieve balance as it hangs. If the piece requires a clasp, decide whether to fabricate or purchase one that is appropriate for the overall design.

If committing to a design with multiple beads and short lengths of chain, such as the one pictured at the beginning of this chapter, fabricate the chain groups in the desired lengths (*see* Chapter 6). If including a clasp in the design, incorporating it at this stage will ensure that the quality of the clasp's finish will correspond to that of the links in the chain. Examine the lengths of chain, file and sand any unwanted irregularities and tumble the chain groups in a barrel polisher. If adding a matt finish to the chain and clasp, it is advisable to do this before beading so that the beads will not be scratched during the finishing process. Other finishes such as oxidation and gold plating can sometimes be done after the beading is completed, depending on what kind of material the beads are made from.

For the beading, you will need snipe-nose pliers, round-nose pliers and flush cutters. If you have an extra pair of snipe-nose pliers, they will make grasping the end of the beading wire easier when wrapping it. Working with beads and wire can be easily done away from the jeweller's bench. Sitting comfortably at a table with good lighting can be more suitable for this type of job. Using a beading mat made of soft fabric can be useful to help organize the beads and prevent them from rolling onto the floor.

Step by Step:
Beading to Embellish a Chain

1. Start by cutting a piece of wire about 6cm long. If the beads have a diameter larger than 7mm, increase the wire length accordingly. Using snipe-nose pliers, make a 90 degree bend about 2 cm from the end.

2. At the bend, using the round-nose pliers, make a loop.

Beading to embelllish a chain – Step 1.

Step 2.

Step 3.

Step 4.

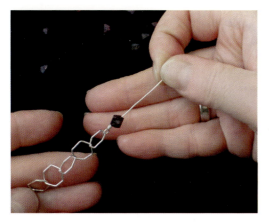

Step 5.

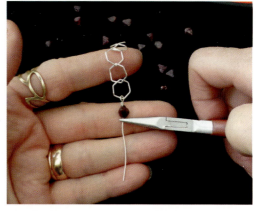

Step 6.

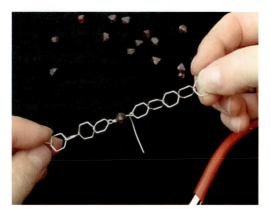

Step 7.

Step 8.

3. Attach it to a link. Holding the loop securely with snipe-nose pliers, wrap the short end of the wire around the base two or three times.

4. Trim the excess wire with the flush cutters as close to the coil as possible and use the snipe-nose pliers to flatten the end of the wire so the coil feels smooth.

5. Thread the bead onto the wire.

6. Holding the wire close to the bead with the tip of the snipe-nose pliers, make a second 90 degree bend.

7. At this bend, make another loop using the round-nose pliers. Attach this to the second chain length.

8. Holding the loop securely with snipe-nose pliers, wrap the remaining wire until you reach the bead. Trim any excess, and flatten any sharp end with the snipe-nose pliers.

ADDING PEARLS OR GEMSTONES TO A DESIGN

The addition of a colourful gem or a soft glowing pearl will provide contrast to the linear aspect of a piece of wire jewellery. Because pearls and most gemstones have a delicate

A freshwater pearl is mounted onto a post and shallow cup setting.

A Tahitian pearl decorates this 18ct gold structural pendant.

finish, care must be taken when working with them. They cannot withstand high temperatures without being damaged. They can also be ruined by harsh procedures such as barrel polishing. These factors make it necessary to set the stone or mount the pearl as the last step in the making process. It is therefore important to consider the setting technique when designing the piece. In the example shown here, a round wire is soldered to the edge of the supporting cup, enabling the setting to be soldered to the surrounding wires of the design.

Pearls

A pearl setting consists of a post, often incorporating a base, which can be a decorative embellishment or a plain shallow cup. An unadorned setting provides a clean, crisp look that can be altered to suit individual designs and is very easy to make. To set a pearl, you will need to source a half-drilled pearl. Start by selecting wire of the correct width for the hole in the pearl, choosing a wire that can be inserted into the hole without using force but which has a fairly snug fit. Determine the depth of the drilled hole and cut a short length of the wire a few millimetres longer than is compatible with the drilled hole. It can then be trimmed to the correct length just before mounting the pearl. You will also need epoxy resin to secure the pearl onto the post: a colourless two-part resin is ideal.

Although a pearl can be set simply on a post, including a base can be both visually pleasing and practical, as a small amount of epoxy can settle into the cup making the bond more secure. Using thin metal sheet, dome a shallow cup to hold the pearl and solder the wire post onto the centre of the cup. Remove any excess solder using needle files before integrating the component into the design.

Setting a pearl in a post – Step 1.

Step 2.

Step 3.

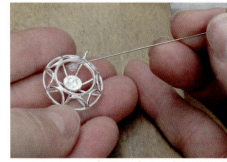

Step 4.

Step by Step: Setting a Pearl in a Post

1. Take a wire of the correct diameter for the hole of the pearl and use a very fine saw blade to make small grooves about a millimetre or two apart along its length. This will allow the resin to provide a more secure connection between the post and the pearl.

2. Solder the post or post and cup setting onto the jewellery piece. Paper away any excess solder and tumble the piece in the barrel polisher. Finish the piece as desired, adding any matt finish or patination at this time.

3. Trim the post to the correct length. The pearl should be set tight against the backing metal.

4. Mix together a small amount of epoxy resin following the manufacturer's instructions. Using a fine pin or other narrow wire instrument, place a small amount of blended resin into the hole of

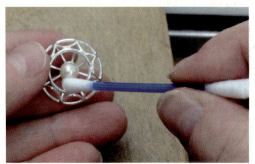

Step 5.

the pearl and onto the post. Only a small drop is necessary as excess will flow out and gather at the base of the pearl.

5. Push the pearl into the post and wipe any excess resin away. Position the piece in a place where it will not be disturbed during drying. If possible, refrain from handling it for twenty-four hours.

When designing different solutions for a cup and post setting, consider how the pearl will sit on the piece and how much the setting needs

A banded agate is set into this pendant using prongs that are integrated into the linear design.

to be integrated into the design. The pearl may be placed in a prominent position or be set back, integrated into the surrounding form. If fabricating a more complicated cup, using hard solder can help with the many soldering steps.

Gemstones

There are many different ways to mount gemstones, including bezel settings and claw settings. Traditional claw settings can be purchased in a range of metals and sizes and integrated into designs. Bezel settings can be sourced ready-made but are most often fabricated in the studio to suit a specific stone. Choosing the most suitable setting will depend primarily on the design of the piece and the size and cut of the stone.

A bezel setting is used to set flat-backed stones called cabochons. A flat base supports a bezel strip that wraps around the outside edge of the stone. This strip is pushed over the top edge of

DIAMONDS AS AN ACCENT

A professional stone setter can assist in setting small diamonds or other tiny gemstones into a design. Micro-pavé setting is a specialist field and a setter can set very tiny stones into a design quickly and securely. When approaching a diamond setter it is advisable to take along a sketch or test piece. You can then discuss the important design details, such as the gauge of wire to be used to fabricate the piece and the size of the stones you desire to set, before making the final piece. Keep in mind that the final cost of setting will depend not only on the size and quality of stones, but also on the total number of stones in the design.

Micro-pavé set diamonds highlight the heart-shaped focal point of this pendant.

This playful Puzzle Ring includes a pearl captured in a cage-like structure.

the stone and rubbed over it to secure the stone in place. Another name for this setting is a 'rub-over' setting.

Setting a stone using a rub-over setting will require support underneath the stone during the burnishing process that secures the stone in the setting. A structural piece of wire jewellery may not be able to support the necessary pressure while burnishing a bezel setting unless a means to support the structure is arranged before setting the stone.

KINETIC ELEMENTS

This term refers to movable parts within pieces of jewellery. In the examples shown here, items suspended inside a wire form can move easily while safely confined within the structure. Smooth spheres such as undrilled pearls work particularly well as they can roll about freely, unhindered by facets and an irregular shape. Beads can also be used, but the visual effect can be marred by the drilled hole on the bead's surface.

A small crystal ball is suspended in this wire-structured pendant.

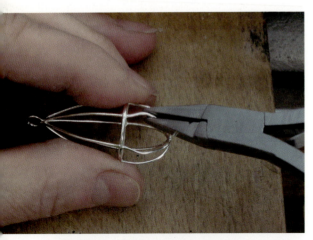

Inserting a sphere into a structural form – Step 1.

Step 2.

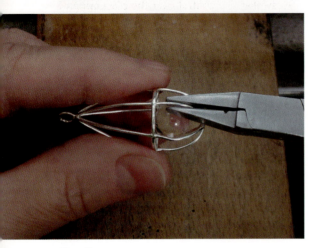

Step 3.

The structural forms can be fabricated in an endless variety of shapes. The important consideration when designing the piece is to be aware of the size of the movable element and the space between the wires that will confine it. You must be able to manipulate the wires, bending them apart for the insertion, and then return the piece to its original form. At the same time, the form must be designed in a manner that will safely hold the embellishment in place. Making a test piece is helpful when deciding the dimensions of the final piece. Creating a matt or oxidized finish or tumbling the final piece to polish it should be done before inserting the movable part.

Step by Step: Inserting a Sphere into a Structural Form

1. Take pliers, preferably ones with rounded edges, and bend two of the structure's wires apart (*see* Chapter 4 regarding customized pliers). Choose an area of the design that will afford the widest opening.

2. Insert the movable element, gently pushing if necessary.

3. Using the pliers, carefully bend the wires back into place. Snipe-nose pliers can be helpful in realigning the wires.

INCORPORATING A HALLMARK

A hallmark consists of a series of marks that are stamped or laser-marked onto precious metal jewellery items. In the UK it is an offence to describe and sell an item as made of precious metal unless it has been hallmarked as such. Certain items, such as those made of silver weighing less than 7.78 grams and gold less than 1 gram, are exempt. Hallmarking provides important information that helps protect the buyer of precious metal objects.

To acquire a hallmark, the piece of jewellery is tested at an assay office to ascertain the quality of precious metal used to make the piece. The outcome of the test will include any solder used in fabrication, so the maker must always use a solder that is of the same grade or above that of the chosen metal. For instance, if using 18ct gold wire to produce a piece of jewellery, it is vital that the solder used is 18ct solder, not 9ct or silver solder. The choice of solder colour or hardness of the solder (easy, medium or hard) will not affect the test results as long as it is of the correct carat.

Hallmarking is done at four locations in the UK: London, Sheffield, Birmingham and Edinburgh. The piece of jewellery is independently tested and three standard marks are applied. The first, a sponsor's mark, or maker's mark, consists of two or three initials set in one of a variety of shields. Each maker's mark is unique as the combination of initials and shield form is never replicated for another maker. The second, a millesimal fineness mark, authenticates the type of metal used and its precious metal content in parts per thousand. For example 18ct gold will be marked with 750 and 9ct gold with 375. The third mark is the individual mark of the assay office with each of the four locations having its own symbol. Two optional marks can be included in the hallmarking process: a letter signifying the year of hallmarking and a traditional fineness mark.

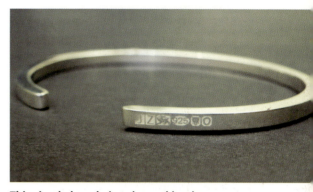

This simple bangle is enhanced by the prominent hallmark.

Before hallmarking, the maker must register with an assay office and choose a sponsor's mark. The cost of a hallmark depends on a variety of factors including the number of items in the packet, the type of jewellery and its size and the speed of service required. A stamped mark, made by striking by hand using a punch and hammer, can be inappropriate for smaller, more delicate items as the force of the strike can deform the metal. Laser hallmarking uses a high-power laser beam to mark the metal and can be an excellent alternative to a traditional struck mark. A great majority of the pieces pictured in this book were hallmarked using a laser.

A jeweller has control over the placement of most hallmarks. Most hallmarks will be located discreetly on the inside or back of a jewellery item. Occasionally, a jeweller will choose to place it in a more prominent position, where it can also function as a form of embellishment. In the example shown here, you can see the sponsor's mark (JZ), the traditional fineness mark for sterling silver, the London assay office mark, the millesimal fineness mark and the date letter (O) which represents the year 2013.

INDEX